COOK-OFF  AMERICA

COOK-OFF  AMERICA

MORE PRIZE-WINNING RECIPES FROM THE PUBLIC TELEVISION SERIES
HOSTED BY MARCEL DESAULNIERS AND CAPRIAL PENCE
PHOTOGRAPHY BY ALEC FATALEVICH

INTRODUCTION

Many food lovers make long journeys visiting the cities and countryside of France, Italy, and even Asia in hopes of discovering and sampling truly great cooking. They can put their passports away because right here in America there are hundreds of food festivals which offer not only great regional cooking, but days of fun-filled festivities. For those who prefer not to travel at all, these festivals can be seen on public television's Cook-off America series, which gives viewers an inside look not only at the festivals, but at the foods and recipes that have made them famous. In this cookbook you will find a collection of recipes from the festivals visited by Cook-off America, including:

Maine Lobster Festival — Every August the 6,000 inhabitants of the scenic oceanside town of Rockland, Maine, welcome more than 100,000 lobster lovers who come to savor their prized seafood and partake in a weekend of entertainment.

National Capital Barbecue Battle — It's not just political dignitaries and activists who can close down Pennsylvania Avenue; every year barbecue zealots armed with tents and grills set up camp on this revered street. It's a friendly takeover as the delicious, irresistible aromas entice thousands of locals to stop work and sample some of the best barbecue in the country.

National Cherry Festival — Those sweet morsels of joy attract more than 500,000 people to Traverse City, Michigan, every year for one of the best food festivals in the country. Visitors find booths brimming with cherry-laden foods, cherry-pie eating contests, crafts, entertainment, and more.

National Chicken Cooking Contest — This contest searches out the best chicken recipes in the country. Fifty-one finalists — one from each state and the District of Columbia — gather together for a two-day cooking marathon where top food experts choose from an astounding array of recipes.

Beaver Creek Pastry Championship — Twelve teams composed of the top pastry chefs in the United States gathered in Beaver Creek, Colorado, and were given nine hours to create seven pastry showpieces.

Asparagus Festival — Every year more than 100,000 asparagus lovers congregate in Stockton, California, to celebrate their beloved vegetable and eat some outrageously delicious asparagus dishes, including the festival's signature dish, Deep Fried Asparagus.

National Beef Cook-Off — Having lost 30 percent of its fat to satisfy health-conscious consumers, beef is back and meat eaters are out of the closet. A nationwide competition searches out the best beef recipes in the United States.

Newman's Own Recipe Contest — Paul Newman is a sensation both on the silver screen and on supermarket shelves where his products have generated more than $100 million for charity. Every year he extends the giving by searching out great home cooks from around the country and giving them a chance to give.

Idaho Spud Day — Potato harvest season in Idaho is kicked off every year with a fun-loving festival that includes a Dutch Oven Cook-off, a free baked potato to everyone attending, and a tug-of-war where the losers end up in a vat of mashed potatoes.

North Carolina BBQ Championship — There may be 25 ways to spell barbecue, but beliefs about what makes it great are countless. North Carolina has its own methods and traditions which are celebrated at the annual Blue Ridge Festival.

Castroville Artichoke Festival — With its rolling hills of artichokes, Castroville, California, is home to a yearly festival where artichokes are battered, fried, sautéed, stewed, steamed, and transformed into everything from soup, pizza, and frittatas to cakes and cookies.

National Pie Championship — However you like your pie — creamy, chunky, nutty, fruity, spicy, berry, chocolate, two-crusted, crumb-crusted, or no-crusted —

you will find it at the National Pie Championship in Orlando, Florida. Pie experts from all over the country roll out their crusts into hopes of winning the grand prize.

Orange Blossom Festival — What is sweet and seedless and was discovered in Riverside, California? The navel orange — celebrated every year at the annual Orange Blossom Festival where visitors pay homage to the first navel orange tree, brought from Brazil in 1870.

California Strawberry Festival — On the map it's simply Oxnard, California, but for many it is "Strawberryland," a magical place where visitors can indulge in baskets of sweet, succulent, heart-shaped berries. The yearly festival offers strawberries in just about every kind of food, from pizza and pie to soup and salad, plus lots of entertainment and crafts.

National Cornbread Festival — The historic town of South Pittsburg, Tennessee, happily closes down Main Street every year to take time to celebrate its beloved cornbread and its vital role in great southern cooking. Thousands of people come, not only for the festivities, but for a chance to compete in the Cornbread Cook-off.

Texas Crab Festival — Blue crabs, with their striking hue, are found along the picturesque coast of Texas. They are the centerpiece attraction at a yearly festival in Crystal Beach which includes a crab cook-off, crab races, and a crab leg contest.

California Avocado Festival — Serious guacamole lovers gather every year in San Diego county, the Avocado Capital of the world, for its renowned festival. Besides guacamole, visitors can find the creamy rich taste of avocado in sandwiches, soup, pies, cakes, and more.

Stonewall Peach Jamboree and Rodeo — It only takes 600 people and a passion for peaches to start a festival that celebrates one of America's favorite fruits. The Texas town swells as thousands of visitors come to enjoy a real southern festival and the tastes of peach pie, peach ice cream, peach cake, and other peachy delicacies.

Gilroy Garlic Festival — Every July the small city of Gilroy gets ready for the annual invasion of more than 200,000 garlic-lovers who consume more than 25,000 pounds of beef, 7,000 pounds of calamari, 26,000 steak rolls, and nearly 6,000 pounds of garlic in just two days. The festival has become one of the biggest summer attractions in California, especially its recipe contest which always turns out mouth-watering garlic delights.

Chuck Wagon Cookoff — Chuck wagon cooking is a treasure of history, tradition, and folklore. The people of Abilene, Texas, have successfully preserved it at a yearly gathering which attracts authentic chuck wagons from all over the country. Some very serious chuck wagon cooks compete in a cookoff which produces delicious, home-cooked food that would keep anyone — on or off the ranch — satisfied.

Memphis in May — Teams practice year-round to compete in the Olympics of barbecue, held, along the Mississippi River every May. Chris Lilly, from the Big Bob Gibson Bar-B-Q team — grand prize winner and one of the most famous teams on the barbecue circuit — comes to the Cook-off America kitchen to reveal barbecue secrets that have been in their family for over 50 years.

The Napa Valley Mustard Festival — Every year wild mustard carpets the Napa Valley vineyards with brilliant hues of green and gold. Mustard is one of the area's most prized commodities and is celebrated at the region's famous late-winter festival. More than 100,000 people come to sample hundreds of different mustards and enjoy mustard-inspired recipes from the best chefs in the region.

Terlingua International Chili Championship and 'Behind the Store' International Chili Cook-off — Terlingua, a remote area of Texas surrounded by desert and mountains, is to chili what Nashville is to country music. For more than 30 years, "chili-heads," with their boundless pride and passion about chili, have gathered there to compete in two world-famous cook-offs.

We hope you enjoy and sample this collection of American regional cooking from all these exciting events and that it brings you many happy hours around the table.

— **Marjorie Poore,** *Producer*

CHOKES AND CLAMS PUTTANESCA

Castroville Artichoke Festival

Richard G. Hansen created this attractive dish in which the artichoke serves as a holder for both the delicious Italian sauce known as "puttanesca" and the tortellini.

Serves 4

Puttanesca
One 28-ounce can crushed tomatoes
One 2 $^{1}/_{4}$-ounce can olives, chopped
One 3-ounce jar capers
One 2-ounce can anchovies, rinsed and chopped
4 medium artichokes, trimmed as for hearts with stems left attached, chopped
One 6 $^{1}/_{2}$-ounce can minced clams
One 10-ounce can whole baby clams
1 teaspoon dried oregano
$^{1}/_{8}$ teaspoon crushed red pepper flakes
Salt, to taste
$^{1}/_{2}$ cup chopped parsley (for garnish)
One 12-ounce package dried tortellini

Artichoke Cups
4 large artichokes
Three 14-ounce cans chicken broth
$^{1}/_{2}$ cup white wine
4 cloves garlic, peeled and smashed
Juice of $^{1}/_{2}$ lemon
Drizzle of olive oil

(continued)

To Make Puttanesca Sauce

1. In a large soup pot or heavy-bottomed skillet, combine tomatoes, olives, capers with juice, anchovies, chopped artichokes, juice from both cans of clams (reserve clams), oregano, and red pepper. Bring to a simmer and cook for approximately five minutes. Season to taste with salt.

To Make Tortellini

1. Cook according to package directions, drain well, and toss with a small amount of olive oil.

To Make Artichoke Cups

1. Trim artichokes by cutting off tops (one to two inches) and removing choke and inner leaves. Cut off stems.
2. In a large skillet, bring chicken broth, wine, garlic, and lemon juice to a simmer. Simmer for 5 minutes. Add trimmed artichokes and cook covered until soft and pliable, approximately ten minutes.

To Serve

1. Place 1 cooked artichoke on a serving plate. Arrange a portion of the cooked tortellini in each artichoke cup and spoon puttanesca sauce over tortellini. Garnish with parsley and serve.

FRIED ARTICHOKES
Castroville Artichoke Festival

Dolores Tottino, Castroville, California. This recipe, for which Castroville is famous, is the most popular item at the festival. Doris is the wife of a second-generation Castroville artichoke grower and daughter of an early farm family.

Serves 10 as an appetizer

1 quart vegetable oil
10 artichokes, cleaned, trimmed, and prepared as for hearts
1 egg
¹/₂ cup milk
1 teaspoon salt
¹/₂ teaspoon garlic salt
¹/₂ cup flour
¹/₂ cup Bisquick mix
¹/₂ teaspoon baking powder
2 tablespoons onion, chopped
2 tablespoons chopped parsley, or parsley flakes

1. Heat oil for deep-frying in a wok, a deep, heavy saucepan, or deep-fryer to 350 degrees.

2. Cut artichokes in halves or quarters, depending upon their size. Set aside.

3. Beat egg and milk in a large bowl. Continue beating while adding salt, garlic salt, flour, Bisquick, and baking powder. Stir in onion and parsley. If batter seems thin, add a little more flour.

4. Add prepared artichokes to batter, coating well. Place coated artichokes in oil and deep-fry, turning, until they are browned. Drain on paper towels, sprinkling with salt, if desired.

CHICKEN CASTROVILLE
Castroville Artichoke Festival

Who can resist sautéed chicken breasts adorned with artichoke hearts, mushrooms, onions, and a light, cream-based cheese sauce? Another favorite from artichoke country, Castroville, California, and a special thank you to its creator, Susan Warne.

Serves 4

4 boneless, skinless chicken breasts
Seasoned flour, for coating
2 tablespoons olive oil
8 ounces cooked artichoke hearts
1 cup sliced mushrooms
$1/_4$ cup diced onions
$1/_4$ white wine
$1/_2$ cup whipping cream
1 cup Jack cheese

1. Lightly coat chicken breasts with flour, shaking off any excess flour.

2. Warm olive oil in a large skillet and sauté chicken breasts over medium-high heat, turning once, until cooked through, about 4 minutes per side. Remove chicken breasts from skillet, drain on paper towels, and keep warm.

3. In the same skillet, sauté the artichoke hearts, mushrooms, and onions until onions are translucent, about 5 minutes. Turn heat to high and carefully pour wine into skillet. Reduce wine by two-thirds. Turn heat to medium, add cream, and reduce cream by one-third.

4. Stir in cheese and allow to melt. Add chicken breasts back to skillet, warm throughly, and serve.

ASPARAGUS BEEF WRAPS
Stockton Asparagus Festival

The sweet and slightly pungent flavors of the marinade make these asparagus-beef bundles a wonderful appetizer for an outdoor party. Pat Resendes was the second place winner in the Adult Appetizers Category at the Stockton Asparagus Festival.

Serves 4

Marinade
1 cup soy sauce
1/2 cup salad oil
1/2 cup sesame chili oil
1/4 cup whiskey
1 1/2 cups brown sugar
3 large garlic cloves, peeled and crushed

1 1/2 pounds chuck or tri-tip steak, cut into thin slices
1 pound asparagus spears, trimmed
3 tablespoons sesame seeds
5 green onions, trimmed and cut thinly on the diagonal

1. Mix together all of the marinade ingredients in a large glass measuring cup with a pour spout. Pour three-fourths of the marinade into a large, airtight container and add meat slices to container. Seal and refrigerate overnight. Pour remaining marinade into a large Ziploc bag and add asparagus. Seal and refrigerate overnight.

2. Remove meat and asparagus from refrigerator and drain. Sauté both in a small amount of vegetable oil in a skillet, or cook on the grill.

3. Wrap each piece of meat around 3 or more spears of asparagus and secure with a toothpick. Place on a serving platter and garnish with sesame seeds and green onion.

Asparagus
Field
Ready to Harvest

DEEP-FRIED ASPARAGUS

Stockton Asparagus Festival

Reprinted from *The Asparagus Festival Cookbook* (Celestial Arts). One of the main attractions at the Stockton Asparagus Festival is the fried asparagus, whose booth always has the longest line. The beer used may be flat, but it livens up the taste of this tempura-like dish.

Serves 6

$^1/_2$ *cup cornstarch*
$^3/_4$ *cup flour*
1 teaspoon salt
1 teaspoon baking powder
$^1/_4$ *teaspoon black pepper*
$^1/_2$ *teaspoon celery salt*
$^1/_2$ *teaspoon baking powder*
2 egg whites
$^2/_3$ *cup cold, flat beer*
3 pounds asparagus spears, trimmed to 8 inches
Peanut oil, for frying

1. With a wire whisk, mix all ingredients excepts except asparagus and peanut oil until well blended.

2. Dip asparagus spears into the batter and deep-fry them in at least 2 inches of peanut oil for 2 minutes, or until golden brown.

ASPARADILLAS
Stockton Asparagus Festival

Reprinted from *The Asparagus Festival Cookbook* (Celestial Arts). This easy-to-prepare "wrap" makes a stunning appetizer. Remember to keep adding an asparagus spear along with strips of red and yellow peppers as you roll up the tortilla.

Makes 50 small appetizers

8 ounces cream cheese, softened
$1/4$ cup mayonnaise
1 tablespoon prepared mustard
10 fajita-sized flour tortillas
2 tablespoons toasted sesame seeds
20 thin deli slices of ham
30 thin asparagus spears, blanched and cooled
10 thin strips each of red and yellow bell pepper

1. Combine cream cheese, mayonnaise, and mustard in a small bowl. Divide mixture evenly between the tortillas, then spread to cover. Sprinkle a small amount of sesame seeds over each tortilla, and top with 2 slices of ham. Place an asparagus spear on the end of each tortilla and begin rolling, adding a yellow and a red pepper strip as you go, as well as 2 more asparagus spears. Roll tortilla completely and fasten with toothpicks. Finish all of the tortillas in the same manner.

2. Cut rolled tortillas into 1-inch pieces to look like pinwheels. Discard ends.

WARM ORIENTAL ASPARAGUS SALAD
Stockton Asparagus Festival

Reprinted from *The Asparagus Festival Cookbook* (Celestial Arts). If you are looking for an interesting and unusual coleslaw, this is a great one to try. The Asian flavors and the warm dressing make it very special.

Serves 6

Salad
1 pound cooked and coarsely shredded
fresh asparagus
2 cups shredded red cabbage
2 cups shredded Napa cabbage
¹/₄ cup diced red onion
¹/₄ cup diced water chestnuts
¹/₄ cup chopped roasted peanuts
¹/₄ cup chopped cilantro
Black sesame seeds, for garnish

Dressing
3 tablespoons vegetable oil
1 tablespoon sesame oil
1 tablespoon soy sauce
1 tablespoon seasoned rice wine vinegar
1 tablespoon dry sherry
1 clove garlic, peeled and pressed

1. Mix all of the salad ingredients except sesame seeds in a large salad bowl.
2. Place all of dressing ingredients in a small saucepan and heat. Pour the hot dressing over the salad ingredients and toss well. Garnish with sesame seeds and serve immediately.

PEACH MANGO GUACAMOLE
California Avocado Festival

1999 First Place, Guacamole Category: Colin McLean
Here's an unusual guacamole made with fresh fruit. The lemon keeps the
avocado from turning brown when the flesh is exposed to air.

Makes 3 to 4 cups

2 avocados, peeled and pitted
Juice of ¹/₂ lemon
1 large ripe peach, peeled and diced
¹/₂ mango, peeled and diced
¹/₂ cup pineapple, diced
³/₄ cup salsa

Mash avocado together with lemon juice in a medium bowl. Add peach, mango,
pineapple, and salsa and gently toss to combine. Serve with chips.

CALIFORNIA AVOCADO AND CHICKEN WRAP

California Avocado Festival

1999 First Place Winner, Sandwich Category: Tim Bridwell
Often supermarkets only carry underripe, hard avocados which are difficult to peel and eat. To ripen them, place in a brown paper bag with an apple and allow to sit at room temperature for a couple of days.

Makes 4 tortillas

1 avocado, peeled and pitted
3 ounces cooked chicken breast, diced or shredded
8 ounces sour cream
8 ounces grated Gruyère cheese
4 large chili-flavored tortillas
Mixed baby greens

1. Warm the tortillas in a non-stick skillet until they are soft and pliable, about 30 seconds.

2. In a bowl, mix together avocado, sour cream, cooked chicken breast, and gruyere cheese until smooth. Divide evenly among the tortillas and garnish each tortilla with a handful of greens. Roll tortillas and serve.

CALIFORNIA AVOCADO POUND CAKE

California Avocado Festival

1999 First Place Winner, Baked Goods Category: Anthony Garcia
The avocado in this cake adds a wonderful texture and flavor which is irresistible. The flavors seem to improve with age, so don't be afraid to make it a day ahead.

Makes 1 cake

1 cup butter or margarine
6 eggs
$^1/_4$ cup Hass avocado flesh
$^3/_4$ cup sour cream
2 $^3/_4$ cups sugar
3 cups all-purpose flour
$^1/_2$ teaspoon salt
$^1/_4$ teaspoon baking soda
$^1/_2$ teaspoon lemon extract
$^1/_2$ teaspoon orange extract
$^1/_2$ teaspoon vanilla extract
Powdered sugar (optional)

Preheat oven to 300 degrees

1. Bring butter or margarine and eggs to room temperature. Grease and flour the bottom and sides of a 10-inch tube pan and set aside.

2. In a small bowl, cream avocado and sour cream. Set aside.

3. In a large mixer bowl, beat the butter or margarine until creamed. Gradually add the sugar and continue to beat until light and fluffy. Add eggs, one at a time, beating about a minute after each egg and 3 more minutes after all of the eggs have been added. Set aside.

4. Stir together the flour, salt, and baking soda. Add flour mixture alternately with the creamed avocado and sour cream to egg mixture, beginning and ending with the flour. Beat well after each addition to the egg mixture. Add lemon, orange, and vanilla extracts and beat thoroughly to combine.

5. Turn batter into prepared pan and bake in oven for 1 hour and 20 minutes, or until a toothpick inserted into the middle comes out clean. Cool for 15 minutes before removing from pan. Once removed, allow pound cake to cool completely. Sprinkle with powdered sugar, if desired.

THE ORIGINAL Q COMPANY BRISKET
National Capital Barbecue Battle

First Place Winner: Wiley McCrary, Atlanta, Georgia

A passion for barbecue has turned Wiley McCrary into a consistent winner and a "circuit" celebrity. He cooks his brisket over a low, indirect fire (220 degrees on a gas grill). His magic number is "190" — the temperature the meat needs to reach before it's done.

Serves 8

One 5–6 pound beef brisket, 75 percent of fat trimmed off

Marinade
3 tablespoons olive oil
3 tablespoons fresh lime juice
2 tablespoons brown sugar
1 tablespoon crushed red pepper flakes
2 cloves garlic, minced

Finishing Glaze
¹/₂ cup barbecue sauce
3 tablespoons honey

1. Place brisket in a container just large enough to hold it. Mix together marinade ingredients and pour over brisket. Place in refrigerator and marinate overnight.

2. To cook: Heat your outdoor grill so it is ready for indirect cooking, or to a temperature of approximately 220 degrees if using a gas grill.

3. Remove brisket from refrigerator and wipe dry (making sure that all of the brown sugar is removed). Place brisket on the grill over indirect heat and cook until the internal temperature of the meat is 160 degrees.

4. Remove brisket from grill, wrap in aluminum foil, return to grill, and cook until internal temperature reaches 190 degrees.

5. Remove meat from grill, and allow to rest for 10 minutes.

6. Make the finishing glaze: combine barbecue sauce and honey and mix well.

7. After resting, cut the meat across the grain into $^1/_4$-inch slices, but leave the bottom 1" of the brisket uncut so you can fan out the slices. Fan out the slices and brush each slice with the finishing glaze.

8. Return the meat to the grill and allow the sauce and meat to heat through. Serve.

DEVAUX FARMS GRILLED LAMB CHOPS
National Capital Barbecue Battle

Brian DeVaux of the "DeVaux Farm Smokers" revealed the secret ingredients used to create this prize-winning recipe, including the ingenious idea of using raspberry jam to give the lamb a wonderful finishing touch. Note that the lamb needs to marinate overnight.

Serves 4

1 tablespoon fresh thyme
1 tablespoon fresh rosemary
1 tablespoon fresh oregano
1 tablespoon fresh basil
2 tablespoons finely chopped fresh garlic
8 lamb loin chops
Olive oil
Salt and pepper, to taste
Seedless raspberry jam

1. Finely chop all of the herbs and place in a small bowl. Add garlic and blend together with herbs. Rub lamb chops with olive oil and then rub herb mixture onto lamb. Season with salt and pepper. Seal the chops in a container and refrigerate overnight.

2. Build a fire in one side of a kettle grill. Remove lamb chops from refrigerator and bring to room temperature. When fire is medium-hot, sear the lamb chops for 2 minutes per side over direct heat, before moving chops to indirect heat. Allow lamb to cook for 8 more minutes. Just before removing lamb from grill, brush lamb chops with raspberry jam. Serve 2 chops per person.

L & L BARBECUED CHICKEN
National Capital Barbecue Battle

Second Place, Chicken Recipe: Larry Hayne, Jonesboro, Georgia
Don't be surprised by the long, slow cooking process recommended here; it's a fiercely guarded conviction on the barbecue circuit that "low and slow" is the key to success. Be sure to start with a whole chicken as too much fat is removed from store-bought chicken parts. The fat is needed for basting during the long cooking process.

Serves 2-4

1 large whole chicken, skin and fat left on, cut into halves or quarters
Salt and freshly ground black pepper, to taste

Basting Sauce
1 cup apple cider vinegar
1 cup vegetable oil
3 tablespoons poultry seasoning

BBQ Sauce
$1/4$ box dark brown sugar
2 tablespoons Heinz 57 Sauce
$1/2$ cup ketchup
3 tablespoons Worcestershire sauce
1 tablespoon fresh lemon juice

1. Prepare your grill for cooking over indirect heat. For a gas grill, the temperature should be 220 degrees.
2. Mix together basting ingredients in a small saucepan and bring to a simmer over medium heat. Simmer for 10 minutes, remove from heat, and allow to cool.
3. Season chicken with salt and pepper. Place on the grill, skin side *down,* and apply basting sauce to both sides of chicken.

4. After 45 minutes, baste again and continue cooking chicken skin side *down*.

5. After 45 minutes, baste again and continue cooking chicken skin side *up*.

6. After 45 minutes, baste again and continue cooking chicken skin side *up*.

7. After 45 minutes, remove chicken from grill, pull off skin.

8. Mix together all of the BBQ sauce ingredients in a small bowl. Set aside.

9. Place chicken on grill and coat with barbecue sauce. Continue cooking for approximately 10 minutes, applying barbecue sauce frequently.

PARADISE RIDGE POTATO SALAD

North Carolina BBQ Championship

Here's a side dish from the Paradise Ridge BBQ Team, the Grand Champion winners of the 2000 North Carolina State Barbecue Championship.

Serves 8–10

6 pounds cooked potatoes (peeled and chopped)
$^1/_2$ cup olives with pimiento
$^1/_2$ cup chopped sweet pickles
$^1/_2$ cup green onions with tops
$^1/_2$ cup red onion, chopped
4 boiled eggs, chopped
2 teaspoons mustard (or to taste)
$^1/_2$ to 1 cup mayonnaise
Salt and pepper, to taste
5–6 red onion slices (optional)

1. Mix together thoroughly the mustard, mayonnaise, salt, and pepper.

2. Place remaining ingredients in a large bowl. Pour mayonnaise mixture on top and mix salad together, taking care not to mash the potatoes.

3. Chill. Add garnish of red onions and serve.

MISSISSIPPI MUD CAKE
North Carolina BBQ Championship

From the Paradise Ridge Competition BBQ Cooking Team
Chocolate, nuts, and marshmallows—who can resist the combination made famous by this Southern cake? There's an extra bonus: it's a "one-bowl" cake that takes little time to prepare.

Makes one 9" x 13" cake

Cake
1 cup butter
$1/2$ cup cocoa
2 cups sugar
4 eggs, slightly beaten
$1^1/2$ cups all-purpose flour
Pinch of salt
$1^1/2$ cups chopped nuts
1 teaspoon vanilla extract
1 10-ounce bag miniature marshmallows

Frosting
One 1-pound box powdered sugar
$1/2$ cup whole milk
$1/3$ cup cocoa
4 tablespoons butter (softened)

Preheat oven to 350 degrees

1. Melt butter and cocoa together and remove from heat.

2. Stir in sugar and beaten eggs and mix well.

3. Add flour, salt, chopped nuts, and vanilla and mix well.

4. Spoon batter into a greased 13 x 9 x 2-inch pan.

5. Bake at 350 degrees for 35–45 minutes until toothpick comes out clean.

6. While cake is baking, start the frosting. In an electric mixer, cream together the butter and one cup of the powdered sugar. Add the cocoa and incorporate. Slowly add the remaining sugar and milk, alternating between each.

7. Sprinkle marshmallows on warm cake.

8. Cover with frosting.

FIESTA ROAST BEEF WITH TROPICAL FRUIT RELISH
National Beef Cook-Off

From Gloria Bradley, 1999 National Beef Cook-Off Grand Prize Winner
Beef tri-tip, which has become very popular, is a boneless roast from the bottom sirloin with a distinctive triangular shape.

Serves 6 to 8

1 package ($1^1/_2$ to 2 pounds) fully cooked beef tri-tip roast
2 cans (8 to $8^1/_4$ ounces each) tropical fruit salad in light syrup
1 large orange
2 to 3 teaspoons spicy brown mustard
$^1/_4$ to $^1/_2$ teaspoon hot pepper sauce
Salt and pepper, to taste
$^1/_2$ cup diced green bell pepper

1. Place beef tri-tip roast (reserving the liquid from the package) in microwave-safe dish. Transfer 3 to 4 tablespoons liquid from package to small saucepan and set aside. Cover roast and microwave on high 7 to 10 minutes or until heated through. Let stand, covered, 5 minutes.

2. Meanwhile drain fruit salad, reserving 3 tablespoons of the syrup. Grate 1 teaspoon peel from orange and set aside. Cut orange in half. Squeeze juice from $1/_2$ orange; peel and chop orange sections from remaining half.

3. Combine reserved syrup, orange juice, mustard, orange peel, pepper sauce, and salt and pepper (as desired) in medium bowl; whisk until blended. Measure $1/_4$ cup of the orange juice mixture and add to beef liquid in saucepan. Set aside. Add reserved fruit, chopped orange, and bell pepper to remaining orange juice mixture in bowl and mix well. Cover and refrigerate.

4. Carve roast across the grain into thin slices. Bring mixture in saucepan to a boil and remove from heat.

5. Arrange beef and fruit relish side-by-side on platter. Spoon hot sauce over beef, as desired. Garnish with orange slices, if desired.

CAESAR SALAD BEEF BURGERS ON GARLIC CROSTINI
National Beef Cook-Off

This recipe transforms America's favorite salad into a burger. The garlic, parmesan, and sourdough add wonderful flavors to the burger.

Serves 4

1¹/₂ *pounds ground beef*
3 cloves garlic, minced
1 teaspoon salt
¹/₂ *teaspoon pepper*
4 romaine lettuce leaves
¹/₄ *cup freshly shaved or grated Parmesan cheese*

Garlic Crostini
8 slices sourdough bread (about 4 x 3 x ¹/₂-inch)
Extra virgin olive oil
2 large cloves garlic, cut lengthwise into quarters

Preheat grill for a medium fire (375 degrees on a gas grill)

1. Combine ground beef, minced garlic, 1 teaspoon salt and ¹/₂ teaspoon pepper in a large bowl, mixing lightly but thoroughly. Lightly shape into four ³/₄-inch patties, shaping to fit the bread slices.

2. Place patties on grill. Cook uncovered for 13 to 15 minutes—turning occasionally— until the internal meat temperature is 160 degrees (juices should show no pink color). Season with salt and pepper, as desired.

3. Meanwhile brush both sides of bread slices lightly with oil. Place bread around outer edge of grill. Grill a few minutes until lightly toasted, turning once. Remove bread slices from grill. Rub both sides of each slice with a garlic quarter.

4. Place one lettuce leaf on four of the bread slices and top each with a burger. Sprinkle evenly with cheese and cover with remaining bread slices. Cut burgers if desired; arrange on lettuce-lined platter, if desired.

SICILIAN GRILL
National Beef Cook-Off

Basil pesto can be purchased in most supermarkets these days, or you may want to try making your own in the food processor with fresh basil, pine nuts, and a good quality olive oil.

Serves 4

8 slices (about 6 x 4 x $^1/_2$-inch thick) firm-textured Italian or Vienna bread
2 to 3 tablespoons prepared Italian (non-creamy) salad dressing (do not use light or reduced-fat)
12 ounces thinly sliced beef salami
4 slices (approximately 4 ounces) provolone cheese
1 jar (7 ounces) roasted red peppers, drained well and patted dry
$^1/_4$ cup prepared basil pesto

1. Brush one side of half of the bread slices with $^1/_2$ of the dressing and place, dressing side down, on a cutting board. Top each bread slice with equal amounts of the pastrami, provolone, and red peppers.

2. Spread one side of the remaining bread slices evenly with the pesto and place pesto side down on top of sandwiches. Brush tops of bread with remaining dressing.

3. Heat a large skillet over medium heat. Place sandwiches in skillet and cook for 2 to 3 minutes per side, or until bread is toasted and cheese is melted. Cut sandwiches in half and serve.

ENDIVE SALAD WITH CHERRIES, ROQUEFORT, AND WALNUTS

National Cherry Festival

This recipe is from the National Cherry Festival and Dr. Myles Bader. This salad tastes better when the dressing is made in advance and chilled thoroughly before adding to endive and lettuce.

Serves 4 to 6

1 small head endive, rinsed and drained
1 small head butter lettuce, rinsed and drained
$^3/_4$ cup walnut oil
3 tablespoons sherry wine vinegar
1 tablespoon lemon juice
Salt and pepper, to taste
$^1/_2$ cup fresh sweet cherries, rinsed and pitted
$^1/_2$ cup walnuts, toasted
4 ounces Roquefort cheese, crumbled
2 tablespoons minced chives

1. Tear endive and lettuce into bite-size pieces and put into a large salad bowl.

2. In a small bowl, whisk together walnut oil, wine vinegar, and lemon juice until well blended; season with salt and pepper.

3. Drizzle dressing over endive and lettuce and toss to coat greens well.

4. Arrange endive and lettuce on 4 to 6 salad plates and top each portion with a serving of cherries, toasted walnuts, Roquefort, and chives.

HOLIDAY CHERRY CHICKEN
National Cherry Festival

This festive and colorful dish is actually dates back hundreds of years to when meats were commonly served with fruits and nuts. From the National Cherry Festival and Dr. Myles Bader.

Serves 4

Chicken
1 (2 1/2 – 3 pound) chicken, cut in pieces and skin removed
3 tablespoons butter or margarine, melted
Salt and pepper, to taste
Paprika, to taste

Cherry Sauce
One 16-ounce can tart cherries, drained and juice reserved
1/2 cup sugar
2 tablespoons cornstarch
1/2 cup chicken broth
1 unpeeled orange, quartered
1/2 cup slivered almonds
Extra orange slices, for garnish (optional)
Toasted almond slivers, for garnish (optional)

To Make Chicken

Preheat oven to 350 degrees

1. Put chicken pieces in a shallow roasting pan and brush with melted butter or margarine. Season both sides of chicken with salt, pepper, and paprika.

2. Place in oven and bake until cooked through (35 to 45 minutes), turning once.

(continued)

To Make Cherry Sauce

1. After reserving ¼ cup of the juice from the cherries, place cherries and remaining juice in a saucepan. Add sugar, stir well, and bring mixture to a boil.

2. Combine reserved cherry juice and cornstarch and mix well to blend. Add to cherry mixture, along with the chicken broth, reduce heat to a simmer, and cook until sauce has thickened. Add orange slices and almonds and remove from heat.

To Assemble

1. Place cooked chicken pieces in a large skillet and pour sauce over chicken. Bring sauce to a simmer and cook for 5 to 10 minutes, warming chicken pieces through.

2. Place on a serving platter and garnish with orange slices and almonds, if desired.

CHERRY TURTLE BROWNIES WITH CHERRY GANACHE

National Cherry Festival

This recipe, a popular item at the festival, was created by Frederick L. Laughlin, department chair of the Northwestern Michigan College Culinary Arts Program. The combination of cherries and chocolate is unbeatable.

Makes one 9 x 13-inch pan of brownies

Brownies
2 cups granulated sugar
1¹/₂ cups butter, softened
3 tablespoons cocoa powder
8 large eggs
¹/₂ teaspoon salt
10 ounces semi-sweet chocolate, melted
¹/₂ cup corn syrup
1 cup sweet cherries, pitted and coarsely chopped
1¹/₂ cups chopped pecans
2 cups all-purpose flour

Ganache
1¹/₂ cups heavy cream
16 ounces semi-sweet chocolate, chopped
¹/₂ cup sweet butter
¹/₄ cup cherry juice concentrate*
¹/₄ cup high-quality kirsch

Topping
12-ounce jar of caramel sauce
Chopped pecans for garnish

(continued)

To Make Brownies

Preheat oven to 350 degrees

1. With a stand mixer, cream together sugar, butter, and cocoa powder in a large bowl. With mixer still running, add 2 eggs at a time, until well blended. Do not overmix.

2. Stir melted chocolate into butter mixture, along with corn syrup and cherries. Stir in pecans and flour until mixture is just blended. Scrape down sides of bowl and mix again.

3. Pour batter into a 9 x 13-inch pan and bake for 45–50 minutes, or until toothpick inserted into the center of brownies comes out clean. Remove from oven and allow brownies to cool.

To Make Ganache

1. Place cream in a heavy saucepan and cook over medium-high heat until a film forms on top of cream. Remove from the heat, add the chocolate and butter and stir to melt until there are no white streaks remaining from the cream. Add the remaining ingredients and stir until a homogenized mixture is formed. Let cool, stirring occasionally.

To Serve

1. Pour cooled ganache over brownies and chill in refrigerator until ganache is firm (about an hour).

2. Warm caramel sauce slightly and drizzle** over ganache layer. Garnish with chopped pecans. Cut and serve brownies.

* *Cherry juice concentrate can be hard to find. If not available through a mail-order source, substitute an additional 1/2 cup of kirsch.*

** *Drizzling suggestions: Dip a fork in the caramel sauce and drizzle it back and forth over the ganache. Or place caramel sauce in a ziploc bag and heat for 10–20 seconds in a microwave until warm. Snip a small corner of the bag and drizzle sauce over ganache.*

CHERRY SLUSH
National Cherry Festival

Italians call it *granita,* French, *granité.* Whatever language, it is a sooth-ing chilled treat which can be served anytime. From the National Cherry Festival and Dr. Myles Bader.

Serves 16

2 cups cherry juice (or blend)
1 cup granulated sugar
2 cups frozen unsweetened tart cherries (or one 16-ounce can unsweetened
  cherries, drained)
One 16-ounce can frozen orange juice, concentrate
2 tablespoons lemon juice
One 2-liter bottle carbonated lemon-lime beverage, chilled

1. In a medium saucepan, combine cherry juice and sugar. Cook over medium heat, stirring frequently, until sugar dissolves and mixture comes to a boil. Reduce heat, simmer for another 3 minutes, and remove from heat.

2. Combine cherries, orange juice concentrate, and lemon juice in a blender or food processor and process for 1 minute or until cherries are puréed.

3. In a 6-cup freezer container, combine juice and sugar mixture with puréed cherries and stir well to combine. Cover tightly and freeze for at least 5 hours or overnight.

4. Remove cherry mixture from freezer 30 minutes before serving. Put ¼ cup cherry slush in each glass, followed by ½ cup of the lemon-lime beverage. Serve immediately (any remaining slush can be refrozen).

JAPANESE AMAZU CHICKEN
National Chicken Cooking Contest

First Place Winner (Michigan): Marie Rizzio, Traverse City, Michigan
This was the National Chicken Cooking Contest's first place winner.
It will "amaze-u" with its succulent fried chicken strips, served over an
Asian-flavored salad.

Serves 4

Amazu Sauce
¹/₄ cup soy sauce
¹/₄ cup sugar
¹/₄ cup rice wine vinegar
1 tablespoon sesame oil

3 large eggs, lightly beaten
³/₄ cup cornstarch
¹/₃ cup vegetable oil
4 boneless, skinless chicken breasts, cut into ¹/₂-inch strips
4 cups fresh bean sprouts
1 small salad cucumber peeled and cut into strips with a vegetable peeler
¹/₃ cup thinly sliced radishes
*3 tablespoons chopped green onion (use only white part, reserving green part for
  garnish)*
Toasted sesame seeds, for garnish
Finely chopped red bell pepper, for garnish

1. To make Amazu Sauce: In a small bowl, mix together soy sauce, sugar, rice wine
   vinegar, and sesame oil. Set aside.

2. In a large bowl, mix together eggs and cornstarch. Set aside.

(continued)

47

3. In a large, nonstick skillet, warm oil over medium-high heat. Dip chicken strips into cornstarch mixture, coating well. Place chicken strips (half at a time) into skillet and cook, turning, for about 5 minutes, or until browned. Drain on paper towels and keep warm.

4. In a large saucepan of boiling water, cook bean spouts for 3 minutes. Drain.

5. Toss bean sprouts, cucumber, radishes, and green onion (white part) together in a large bowl and spread onto a serving dish.

6. Arrange chicken strips on top of vegetables and drizzle with Amazu Sauce. Sprinkle with toasted sesame seeds, red bell pepper, and green onions (green part). Serve.

TEA SMOKED CHICKEN WITH SESAME VEGETABLE RELISH

National Chicken Cooking Contest

Second Place Winner (California): Roxanne Chan, Albany, California
If you love the flavors of smoked food and never tried doing it yourself, this recipe is a perfect starter as it comes together quite simply right on your stovetop. For an attractive presentation, slice the chicken diagonally and serve over a mound of relish.

Serves 4

4 boneless, skinless chicken breasts

Sesame Vegetable Relish
2 tablespoons sesame oil
2 tablespoons seasoned rice vinegar
2 cloves garlic, peeled and crushed
2 teaspoons soy sauce
$1/2$ teaspoon crushed red pepper flakes
$1/2$ teaspoon grated orange peel
4 tablespoons finely diced water chestnuts
4 tablespoons finely diced red bell pepper
4 tablespoons finely diced carrot
4 tablespoons finely diced celery
2 tablespoons chopped cilantro
2 small green onions, minced

Smoking Mixture
$1/4$ cup raw rice
$1/4$ cup molasses
$1/4$ cup brown sugar
$1/4$ cup black tea leaves
1 cinnamon stick
1 tablespoon whole allspice
Sesame seeds, for garnish

1. In a medium bowl, mix together all of the relish ingredients. Refrigerate.

2. Line a wok or a heavy-bottomed stockpot with aluminum foil. On top of foil, place rice, molasses, brown sugar, tea leaves, cinnamon stick, and allspice berries. Stir gently.

3. Place a small rack over smoking mixture and place chicken breasts on rack. Cover stockpot tightly and cook over a medium-high heat for 10 minutes. Remove from heat and let sit, covered, another 10 minutes.

4. Remove chicken breasts and slice. Place relish on a serving dish and arrange chicken slices on top. Sprinkle with toasted sesame seeds and serve.

MANDARIN CHICKEN WRAPS
National Chicken Cooking Contest

Fourth Place Winner (Utah): Ruth Kendrick, Ogden, Utah
It is really not surprising that Asian-style recipes, with their bold and complex flavors, dominated all the top prize winners at the National Chicken Cooking Contest. This wrap is especially delightful and makes a wonderful midday meal.

Serves 8

1 cup light soy sauce
1 tablespoon cornstarch
2 teaspoons grated fresh ginger
4 boneless, skinless chicken breasts, cut into thin strips
Eight 11-inch flour tortillas
2 tablespoons vegetable oil
$^1/_4$ teaspoon crushed red pepper flakes
2 cloves garlic, minced
1 medium onion, peeled and sliced
3 cups coleslaw mix*
1 red bell pepper, cored and cut into thin strips
1 bunch of chives
1 small bunch of fresh cilantro, washed and dried well
Prepared plum sauce
Prepared sweet and sour sauce

Pre-heat oven to 300 degrees

1. In a glass dish, mix together soy sauce, cornstarch, and ginger. Add chicken strips, stirring to coat. Marinate in refrigerator for 15 minutes.

2. Wrap tortillas in aluminum foil and place in oven for 15 minutes to warm.

3. In a large fry pan, warm oil over a medium-high heat. With a slotted spoon, remove chicken from marinade, drain, and place in fry pan. Sprinkle chicken with red pepper

flakes and garlic and stir-fry for 2 minutes. Add onion, 1 cup of the coleslaw mix, and red pepper strips and continue stir-frying about 3 minutes more, or until chicken is no longer pink.

4. On each of the warmed tortillas, place remaining coleslaw mix in equal portions. Top with equal portions of the chicken mixture. Roll tortillas, then slice diagonally through the middle and tie with a piece of chive. Arrange wraps on a bed of the cilantro and serve with warmed or room temperature plum and sweet and sour sauces.

* *Coleslaw mix can be found in the fresh produce (salad) departments of most supermarkets.*

BOB'S CHAMPIONSHIP CHILI RECIPE
Terlingua International Chili Championship

First Place Winner, Chili Category: Bob Coats
This recipe uses a cooking technique that is favored by many chili champions — that of layering spices, i.e. adding in a new set every 30 to 60 minutes. Don't be surprised that there are no beans in this chili. True "chiliheads" do not use any beans or vegetables in their chili.

Serves 8

2$^1/_2$ pounds cubed beef chuck
1 tablespoon vegetable shortening
2 cups beef broth
1 cup chicken broth
2 Serrano chili peppers

First Spices
2 teaspoons granulated onion
$^1/_2$ teaspoon cayenne
2 teaspoons beef bouillon granules
$^1/_4$ teaspoon salt
2 teaspoons chicken bouillon granules
1 tablespoon light chili powder
2 tablespoons red chili powder

Second Spices
2 teaspoons ground cumin
2 teaspoons granulated garlic
$^1/_4$ teaspoon hot sauce
2 tablespoons chili powder
1 tablespoon light chili powder
1 packet Sazon Goya

(continued)

Third Spices

1 tablespoon chili powder
1 teaspoon ground cumin
$^1/_4$ teaspoon granulated garlic
$^1/_4$ teaspoon cayenne
$^1/_4$ teaspoon brown sugar

1. In a large, heavy pot, brown beef in shortening. Drain fat from pan.

2. Add beef broth, chicken broth, and tomato sauce. Stir to combine, and float chilies on top. Bring meat mixture to a boil and add first set of spices. Reduce heat to a simmer, cover, and cook for 1 hour, stirring occasionally.

3. After an hour remove chilies, squeeze their liquid back into mixture, and add second set of spices. Add more chicken broth if mixture is getting dry. Bring mixture back to a simmer, cover, and cook for another 30 minutes, stirring occasionally.

4. Add third set of spices and simmer an additional 10 minutes. Correct salt, cayenne, and chili powder to taste.

BUD'S BEANS
Terlingua International Chili Championship

Second Place Winner, Beans Category: Marion J. "Bud" Barrick
Many people might call this recipe "chili," but at the Chili Championship, it belongs in the bean category. Chorizo is a highly seasoned, ground pork sausage that adds lots of flavor to this dish.

1 pound ground beef
2 chorizo sausages, casings removed
1 large onion, chopped
2 cloves garlic, peeled and slivered
One 10-ounce can tomato sauce
One 14$^1/_2$-ounce can diced tomatoes
83 ounces canned pinto beans (one 55-ounce can plus one 28-ounce can)
3$^1/_4$ cups water
3 tablespoons chili powder
$^1/_2$ tablespoon cumin
1 tablespoon salt

1. In a large, heavy skillet, brown the ground beef, sausage, onion, and garlic until meat is crumbly. Drain off grease and place meat mixture in an 8-quart pot.

2. Add remaining ingredients to pot, bring to a boil, reduce heat to a simmer, and cook about 1$^1/_2$ hours. Add more water if liquid runs dry.

HOT WINGS
Terlingua International Chili Championship

This winning recipe by Jack Ware comes from the "hot wings" competition at Terlingua, Texas. The wings are deep fried and then allowed to sit in a savory and spicy sauce. They make a hearty appetizer.

3 pounds chicken wings

Flour Mixture
2 to 3 cups all-purpose flour
$1^1/_2$ teaspoons seasoning salt
1 teaspoon black pepper
1 teaspoon ground rosemary
1 teaspoon crushed or ground chicken bouillon granules

Peanut or canola oil, for frying

Sauce Mix
8 tablespoons (1 stick) butter
$^1/_2$ cup hot sauce (or to taste)
2 teaspoons apple cider vinegar
1 tablespoon honey
1 teaspoon Worcestershire sauce

1. Rinse and trim the chicken wings. Cut each wing into 3 pieces and discard the tips. Leave chicken wings moist.

2. Mix together all of the flour mixture ingredients in a large bowl. Put chicken wings into flour mixture, toss to coat, and allow to sit for 15 minutes in the refrigerator.

3. Heat oil to 400 degrees. Shake excess flour off of wings and deep-fry for about 10 to 12 minutes, or until golden brown. Drain on paper towels.

4. Melt butter in a small saucepan and add the rest of the sauce ingredients. Bring to a boil and turn heat to low to keep sauce warm.

5. Place chicken wings in a container just large enough to hold them. Pour sauce over chicken wings and let sit for at least 15 minutes before serving.

CACTUS CHILI
Terlingua International Chili Championship

First Place: James Barker, Crosby, Texas.

Serves 6 to 8

1 tablespoon vegetable oil
2 pounds mock tenderloin (similar to a shoulder steak) cut into $^3/_8$-inch cubes
1 teaspoon seasoning salt
$^1/_4$ cup brown sugar
One 8-ounce can tomato sauce
One 14$^1/_2$-ounce can beef broth
1 teaspoon beef bouillon granules
2 tablespoons plus $^1/_2$ teaspoon onion powder
1 tablespoon plus 1 teaspoon garlic powder
$^1/_2$ teaspoon cayenne pepper
1 teaspoon chicken bouillon granules
6 tablespoons plus 1 teaspoon dark chili powder
$^1/_2$ teaspoon minced jalapeño pepper
$^1/_2$ teaspoon black pepper
2 teaspoons ground cumin
$^1/_8$ teaspoon salt

1. Heat oil in a heavy 3-quart saucepan. Add meat cubes, seasoning salt, and brown sugar; allow meat to brown.

2. Mix together tomato sauce, beef broth, beef bouillon granules, 2 tablespoons of the onion powder, 1 tablespoon of the garlic powder, cayenne, chicken bouillon granules, 2 tablespoons of the dark chili powder, and jalapeño pepper. Pour over meat, stir well to combine, turn heat to medium, and simmer for 1$^1/_2$ hours, partially covered.

3. Combine 4 tablespoons of the dark chili powder, remaining onion powder, remaining garlic powder, and black pepper and pour into meat mixture. Bring mixture to a boil, reduce to a simmer, and simmer 15 minutes longer.

4. Add cumin powder, salt, and last teaspoon of dark chili powder to meat and stir to combine. Simmer 15 minutes longer and serve.

JALAPEÑO CORNBREAD

"Behind the Store" International Chili Cook-off

Cornbread is the traditional accompaniment to chili, especially a rich and tasty one like this recipe.

Serves 8

2 teaspoons butter
1 cup yellow corn meal
$^{3}/_{4}$ teaspoon salt
$^{1}/_{2}$ teaspoon baking soda
1 cup buttermilk
2 eggs, beaten
1 can cream-style corn
1 medium onion, chopped
4 to 6 canned jalapeños, chopped
6 ounces cheddar cheese, shredded

Preheat oven to 350 degrees

1. Melt butter in a 9- to 10-inch cast iron skillet.

2. Combine corn meal, salt, and baking soda in a bowl. In another bowl, mix together remaining ingredients. Add corn meal mixture to liquid mixture and stir just to blend. Add melted butter and stir until blended.

3. Pour batter into skillet and place in oven. Bake for 45 to 60 minutes, or until tooth pick inserted in the middle comes out clean. Serve with additional cheese on top, if desired.

63

WHITE CHOCOLATE ICE CREAM
"Behind the Store" International Chili Cook-off

The best way to finish off a meal of chili is with a cool, soothing dish of ice cream. This is a favorite of our host, Marcel Desaulniers, famous for his *Death by Chocolate* series of books. Caution: you may never want to eat store-bought ice cream again after eating this.

---

8 ounces white chocolate, chopped
$^1/_2$ cup half-and-half
$2^1/_4$ cups heavy cream
$^3/_4$ cup sugar
4 egg yolks

1. Heat the white chocolate and half-and-half together in the top half of a double boiler over medium-low heat, stirring until completely melted and smooth, about $6^1/_2$ to 7 minutes.

2. Heat the heavy cream and $^1/_4$ cup granulated sugar in a medium saucepan over medium-high heat. When hot, stir to dissolve the sugar. Bring to a boil.

3. While the heavy cream mixture is heating, place $^1/_2$ cup granulated sugar and 4 egg yolks in the bowl of an electric mixer fitted with a paddle. Beat on high speed for 4 until slightly thickened and pale yellow, stopping occasionally to scrape down the bowl.

4. Gradually pour the boiling heavy cream mixture into the beaten sugar and egg yolk mixture and mix on low to combine, about 45 seconds.

5. Return the combined mixture to the saucepan. Heat over medium heat, stirring constantly. Bring to a temperature of 185 degrees, about $2^1/_2$ minutes.

6. Remove from the heat and transfer to a large stainless steel bowl. Add the white chocolate and half-and-half mixture and stir to combine.

7. Cool in an ice-water bath to a temperature of 40 to 45 degrees.

8. Freeze in an ice-cream freezer following the manufacturer's instructions.

9. Transfer the semifrozen ice cream to a plastic container, securely cover the container, then place in the freezer for several hours before serving. Serve within 4 days.

BUTTERMILK BISCUITS
Chuck Wagon Cookoff/Western Heritage Classic

Reprinted from *Texas Cowboy Cooking* by Tom Perini (Time-Life Books). Biscuits have always been a mainstay of chuck wagon cooking — in fact, a good cook is judged by the how tender and light his biscuits are. Tom Perini's are some of the best.

Makes 24 biscuits

2 cups flour
2 teaspoons baking powder
$^1/_2$ teaspoon baking soda
$^3/_4$ teaspoon salt
3 tablespoons vegetable shortening
1 cup buttermilk

Preheat oven to 450 degrees

1. Combine the dry ingredients.

2. Add the shortening and mix well with the back of a mixing spoon.

3. Add the buttermilk and mix thoroughly.

4. Roll out dough on a floured board to a $^1/_2$-inch thickness.

5. Cut into rounds and place on an ungreased baking sheet.

6. Bake for about 10 minutes, or until golden brown.

TRAIL-BLAZIN' BEEF STEW
Chuck Wagon Cookoff/Western Heritage Classic

One of the highlights of our trip to Abilene, Texas, was meeting Tom Perini, who has put chuck wagon cooking on the map with his restaurant, The Perini Ranch Steakhouse, and his cookbook, *Texas Cowboy Cooking,* published by Time-Life Books. This is one of the book's delicious offerings.

Serves 6 to 8

6 tablespoons olive oil, divided in half
2 pounds boneless chuck or pot roast, trimmed and cut into 1-inch cubes
1 teaspoon garlic powder, divided in half
2 teaspoons ground cumin, divided in half
2 large white onions, cut into 8 pieces each
5 cups beef stock
3 cups water
3 cloves garlic, minced
9 large red potatoes, cut in half
4 ears corn, cut into fourths
2 carrots, peeled and cut into 1-inch chunks
$^1/_2$ cup coarsely chopped cilantro
1 teaspoon salt
$^1/_2$ teaspoon ground black pepper
Flour tortillas for serving

1. Heat 3 tablespoons of the oil in a large skillet. Stir-fry meat, garlic powder, and cumin.
2. Remove with slotted spoon and put meat in a 6- or 8-quart stockpot.
3. Add the onions to the skillet with the remaining 3 tablespoons of oil and sauté until soft.
4. Transfer to the stockpot with the meat.
5. Add all the remaining ingredients to the stockpot and bring to a boil.
6. Cover, reduce heat, and simmer 1$^1/_2$ to 2 hours, stirring occasionally.
7. Add beef stock, as needed
8. Serve with flour tortillas.

PEACH COBBLER
Chuck Wagon Cookoff/Western Heritage Classic

Think of a cobbler as an upside-down pie with a biscuit topping. Cobblers are also known as grunts, slumps, or spoon pies. For a unique variation, replace one cup of the peach slices with one cup of fresh blueberries.

Serves 8

$^1/_2$ recipe of buttermilk biscuit batter (see page 67)

5 cups peach slices (fresh, frozen, or canned)
1 tablespoon cornstarch
$^2/_3$ cup sugar
2 tablespoons lemon juice
$^1/_2$ cup water

Preheat oven to 400 degrees

1. Lightly grease a 9 x 13-inch baking dish or casserole.

2. Combine cornstarch, sugar, lemon juice, and water in bowl and mix well. Add peaches and mix again. Place fruit mixture in baking dish and cook for 10 minutes. Remove from oven.

3. Increase the heat of the oven to 450 degrees.

4. Pour the biscuit batter over the warm fruit and return to oven.

5. Bake for about 10 minutes, or until golden brown.

GOLDEN APPLE SPICE CORNBREAD

National Cornbread Festival

Second Place Winner, 4-H Category: Becca Blevins, South Pittsburg, Tennessee

Cornbread is traditionally made in heavy cast iron skillets which are heated before the batter is added. Lodge Cast Iron, also in South Pittsburg (www.lodgemfg.com), makes them in every size and shape imaginable.

Serves 12

$1^2/_3$ cups cornmeal
2 cups milk
1 egg
3 tablespoons sugar
$^3/_4$ tablespoon cinnamon
1 apple, peeled, cored, seeded, and diced
4 tablespoons raisins
$^1/_2$ cup vegetable oil

Preheat oven to 450 degrees

1. In a large bowl mix together cornmeal, milk, and egg.
2. In a small bowl, combine sugar and cinnamon and add to cornmeal mixture along with chopped apple, raisins, and oil.
3. Stir gently and pour into a 9-inch cast iron skillet.
4. Place skillet in oven and bake for 45 minutes, or until golden brown.

CORNBREAD SUPREME
National Cornbread Festival

First Place Winner: Kay Gay and Helen Hollansworth, Gulf Shores, Alabama
Great for a Sunday supper or as lunch served with a green salad, this dish
would also be good for brunch with a fruit salad.

Serves 8

3 pieces thick-sliced bacon
4 eggs
1 package Martha White's Yellow Cornbread Mix
¹/₄ cup milk
1 stick butter, melted and cooled
6 dashes hot sauce
1 medium onion, peeled and coarsely chopped
One 1-ounce package frozen spinach, thawed and squeezed of all liquid
1 pound fresh shrimp, peeled, deveined, cooked, and coarsely chopped
2 cups finely grated cheddar cheese
Chopped parsley, for garnish

Preheat oven to 375 degrees

1. In a 10-inch skillet, fry bacon until crisp. Remove from pan, cool, and crumble for
   garnish. Set aside. Pour off excess grease from skillet and wipe with a paper towel,
   leaving just enough grease to coat sides and bottom of skillet. Place skillet in preheated oven.

2. With an electric mixer, beat eggs until fluffy in a large bowl. Add cornbread mix,
   milk, butter, and hot sauce, stirring with a wooden spoon until just blended. Mix in
   onion, spinach, shrimp, and 1¹/₂ cups of the cheddar cheese, stirring to just combine
   ingredients.

3. Remove skillet from oven and pour batter into hot skillet. Top with remaining ¹/₂ cup
   of cheddar cheese. Place skillet back in oven and bake for 30 minutes, or until toothpick comes out clean.

4. Remove skillet from oven and garnish with crumbled bacon and parsley. Cut into
   8 wedges and serve.

MARCEL DESAULNIERS' FEROCIOUS FRIED CHICKEN

National Cornbread Festival

We figured if anyone can make a good fried chicken, it would be our host Marcel Desaulniers, whose world-famous Trellis restaurant is in Williamsburg, Virginia. His chicken turned out better than "good" with everything you expect in fried chicken — a delectable, crispy coating protecting some warm, juicy meat.

Serves 2-4

1 chicken, cut into pieces
1 cup buttermilk
³/₄ cup cornmeal
³/₄ cup flour
Salt
Fresh cracked black pepper
Oil for frying (peanut or vegetable)

Preheat oven to 350 degrees

1. Season the chicken pieces with salt and freshly cracked black pepper.

2. Dip chicken pieces in buttermilk, coating thoroughly.

3. Combine the cornmeal and flour in a shallow dish. Roll the chicken pieces in the mixture, coating thoroughly.

   Note: for extra crispy chicken, repeat steps 2 and 3.

4. Pour cooking oil into a large frying pan to a depth of half an inch. Heat over medium-high heat until very hot.

5. Add chicken pieces to hot oil and cook until golden brown. The hot oil should reach half-way up the sides of the chicken. Turn chicken and cook on second side.

6. When chicken pieces are completely browned, remove from pan and place on baking sheet. Continue cooking chicken in oven until chicken is done.

OKRA FUNGEE
National Cornbread Festival

Reprinted from *Burger Meisters* by Marcel Desaulniers (Simon & Schuster). Okra, also known as "ladies' fingers," is a vegetable with green pods commonly found in the South where it is used in soups and stews. If you can't find fresh okra, frozen is the next best choice.

Serves 4

1 cup yellow cornmeal
2$^1/_2$ cups cold water
1$^1/_2$ teaspoons salt
$^1/_2$ teaspoon white pepper
Pinch cayenne pepper
1$^1/_4$ cups stemmed and sliced ($^1/_4$-inch thick) fresh okra
4 tablespoons unsalted butter

1. In a small stainless steel bowl, combine the cornmeal with 1 cup cold water.
2. Heat the remaining 1$^1/_2$ cups water with the salt, white pepper, and cayenne pepper in a 2-quart saucepan over high heat. Bring to a boil, then add the okra and cook for 2 minutes. Add the cornmeal–water mixture. Bring the mixture to a boil, then reduce the heat to medium-low. Continue cooking, stirring constantly, until the mixture releases itself from the sides of the pan, about 3 to 4 minutes. Stir in the butter and serve immediately.

CREAMY CORN AND CRAB CHOWDER
Texas Crab Festival

Doug Head, High Island High School, from the *Texas Crab Festival Cookbook* (Boliver Peninsula Chamber of Commerce). We modified the original version of this recipe by adding fresh corn kernels as crab and corn are a traditional combination. Try to use fresh crabmeat; it's well worth the extra cost.

Serves 2

1 large yellow onion, chopped
1 large potato, peeled and chopped
1 stalk celery, sliced thin
1 carrot, peeled and sliced thin
1 ear fresh corn kernels, removed from cob
$^1/_2$ teaspoon dried thyme, crumbled
$^1/_2$ teaspoon dried basil, crumbled
$1^1/_2$ cups water
1 cup skim milk
2 tablespoons flour
$^1/_8$ teaspoon cayenne
$^1/_2$ pound crabmeat
2 tablespoons chopped fresh parsley

1. In a medium-sized heavy saucepan, combine onion, potato, celery, carrot, thyme, basil, and water. Bring contents of saucepan to a simmer and cook, uncovered, for 15 minutes.

2. In a small bowl, blend the milk, flour, and cayenne pepper until smooth. Stir into the vegetable mixture, bring contents of saucepan back to a simmer, and cook, stirring constantly, for another 3 minutes.

3. Add the crabmeat and cook another 5 minutes. Place chowder in soup bowls and garnish with chopped parsley.

CRYSTAL BEACH CRAB CAKES
Texas Crab Festival

Kaye Land, from the *Texas Crab Festival Cookbook* (Boliver Peninsula Chamber of Commerce). There are probably as many ways to make crab cakes as there are chefs, but always keep in mind that the crab meat should be the star player.

Serves 4

1 egg
2 teaspoons Dijon mustard
2 tablespoons mayonnaise
$1/2$ teaspoon Worcestershire sauce
$1/4$ cup minced red pepper
1 pound fresh lump crabmeat
$1 1/2$ cup fresh bread crumbs
Salt and freshly ground pepper, to taste
4 teaspoons butter
Lemon wedges
Homemade tartar sauce

1. Combine the egg, mustard, mayonnaise, Worcestershire sauce, and red pepper in a bowl and mix well. Add the crabmeat and $1/3$ cup of bread crumbs and mix gently.

2. With a $1/3$ cup measuring cup, portion out crab mixture and shape into 8 patties. Patties should be about 3 inches in diameter.

3. Combine the remaining bread crumbs, curry powder, and salt and pepper in a shallow dish. Coat the crab patties with the bread crumb mixture, gently reshaping patties as they are placed onto a baking sheet. Chill for 30 minutes.

4. Coat a nonstick skillet with cooking spray and heat the skillet over a medium heat. Add 2 teaspoons of the butter, swirling the skillet until the butter melts. If you are not using a nonstick skillet, you may need more butter. Add 4 of the patties and cook for 4 minutes per side, or until golden brown.

5. Remove patties to a heated plate and repeat the process with the remaining butter and patties. Top cooked patties with lemon wedges and serve with tartar sauce.

CRAB COQUILLE

Texas Crab Festival

This recipe comes from Shirley Adams of Crystal Beach, Texas, famous for its blue crabs. If you are lucky enough to find these small blue crabs, use their cooked shells as a decorative serving dish.

Serves 6

2 tablespoons butter or margarine, melted
1¹/₂ cups bread crumbs
1¹/₂ cups mayonnaise
¹/₃ cup minced celery
¹/₄ cup finely shredded Swiss cheese
¹/₄ cup sherry
1 tablespoon chopped fresh parsley
1 clove garlic, minced
¹/₂ teaspoon paprika
Pinch of white pepper
8 ounces (1 cup) fresh lump crabmeat
Fresh parsley sprigs, for garnish

1. Lightly oil 6 ovenproof shells or individual shallow baking dishes. Set in a 15¹/₂ x 10¹/₂-inch jelly roll pan. Set aside.

2. In a small bowl, mix butter or margarine with ¹/₂ cup of the bread crumbs and set aside.

3. In a medium bowl, mix together remaining 1 cup of bread crumbs with the mayonnaise, celery, cheese, sherry, parsley, garlic, paprika, and pepper. Break up crabmeat and stir into mayonnaise mixture. Spoon into shells or baking dishes and sprinkle with buttered bread crumbs.

4. Turn on broiler. Broil shells or baking dishes 6 inches from the heat source for 2 to 4 minutes, or until golden brown and bubbly. Garnish with parsley sprigs and serve immediately.

CALAMARI WITH TOMATO SAUCE

Gilroy Garlic Festival

This signature dish from the Gilroy Garlic Festival was created by head chef Val Filice. Be sure not to overcook the calamari (squid) or it will become rubbery.

Serves 6 to 8

Red Sauce
1 pound whole, peeled tomatoes, canned or fresh
1 tablespoon olive oil
$^1/_2$ green pepper, chopped
1 stalk celery, chopped
1 medium-sized yellow onion, chopped
2 cloves fresh garlic, minced

Calamari
3 pounds calamari, cleaned and cut
$^1/_3$ cup olive oil
$^1/_4$ cup white sherry
1 tablespoon crushed fresh garlic
$^1/_2$ lemon
1 teaspoon dry basil or 1 tablespoon fresh
1 teaspoon dry oregano or 1 tablespoon fresh
$^1/_4$ teaspoon dry crushed red pepper

(continued)

To make the red sauce

1. Mash tomatoes with potato masher and set aside.

2. In medium-sized pan heat oil, add chopped ingredients, and sauté until onion is transparent.

3. Add mashed tomatoes and simmer for a half hour.

To make calamari

1. In large skillet heat olive oil at high heat.

2. Add wine and sherry and sauté crushed garlic.

3. Squeeze the juice of $^1/_2$ lemon into pan and place lemon rind in pan.

4. Sprinkle herbs over and add calamari.

5. Sauté calamari for approximately 4 minutes on high heat. Do not overcook.

To assemble and serve

Pour red sauce over calamari, heat for 1 minute, and serve.

MARRIAGE PROPOSAL CHICKEN

Gilroy Garlic Festival

Jim Baggese, the creator of this mouthwatering recipe, received a marriage proposal from a visitor to the Garlic Festival who said, "Anyone who cooks that good I want to marry." When you try it, you'll see why.

Serves 4

1 chicken (cut in pieces)

Marinade
$^1/_4$ cup red wine
1 tablespoon lemon juice
2 tablespoons olive oil
$^1/_2$ teaspoon fresh rosemary
$^1/_4$ cup beer
$^1/_2$ teaspoon pepper
1 teaspoon seasoned salt
$^1/_2$ teaspoon oregano
$^1/_2$ teaspoon Italian spices
1 tablespoon crushed garlic (or more to taste)

1. Combine all marinade ingredients into a bowl. Whisk until well combined.

2. Pour marinade over chicken pieces and allow to marinate, preferably overnight in the refrigerator.

3. Prepare the fire on your grill and cook the chicken over indirect heat for approximately 30–45 minutes, or until juices run clear.

PEPPER BEEFSTEAK SANDWICHES

Gilroy Garlic Festival

Before every festival, Chef Lou Trinchero orders up 25,000 pounds of beef to feed the garlic-hungry visitors who descend on Gilroy during festival time looking for these mouth-watering sandwiches.

Serves 8

Garlic Butter
$^1/_2$ cup (one stick) of softened butter
2 cloves garlic, minced (or more to taste)

Sandwiches
8 bell peppers, seeded and sliced in quarters
1 medium-sized onion, chopped
3 cloves fresh garlic, minced
Salt and pepper to taste
Olive oil
2 pounds top sirloin steak
8 French rolls, halved

1. Stir softened butter and minced garlic together until well combined. Set aside.
2. Season steak with salt and pepper. Place on a grill and cook to desired doneness.
3. In a skillet, sauté peppers, onion, garlic, and salt and pepper in olive oil until tender.
4. Brush rolls with garlic butter and heat on the grill until toasted lightly.
5. Slice steak thinly and place on bottom half of roll.
6. Top with pepper–garlic mixture on other half of roll.

CREAMY POTATO GRATIN WITH GORGONZOLA, PEARS, AND PECANS

Gilroy Garlic Festival

Camilla Saulsbury of Bloomington, Indiana, was a first-prize winner at the 2000 Garlic Festival in Gilroy with this unusual and delicious potato gratin.

Serves 6

10 large garlic cloves, peeled
$^1/_3$ cup Marsala wine
$1^1/_4$ cups heavy cream
3 large Russel potatoes ($1^1/_2$ pounds), peeled and thinly sliced
2 large pears, peeled, cored, and thinly sliced
Salt and freshly cracked pepper
8 ounces Gorgonzola cheese, crumbled
1 cup pecans, lightly toasted and chopped
1 tablespoon fresh rosemary, chopped

Preheat over to 400 degres

1. In a small pan filled with water, parboil the garlic cloves until tender, about 8 minutes.
2. Place cloves and Marsala in a blender; purée until smooth. Combine with cream and set aside.
3. Lightly grease an oval au gratin dish or rectangular glass dish and arrange one-third each of the potatoes and pears. Dot potatoes with one-third of the Gorgonzola and sprinkle with a little salt and pepper. Top with one-third cup pecans and 1 teaspoon rosemary. Repeat layering two more times. Pour garlic–cream mixture over top.
4. Bake, covered with foil, for 25 minutes. Remove foil and bake 20 to 35 minutes longer or until almost all of the cream mixture is absorbed and the potatoes are tender.

CRISPY GARLIC SALMON CAKES WITH ROASTED CORN SALSA

Gilroy Garlic Festival

Susan Runkle of Walton, Kentucky, beat some stiff competition at the Garlic Festival with these tasty salmon cakes, which placed second. They make an excellent appetizer or luncheon dish.

Serves 6

Salmon Cakes

10 ounces small red potatoes (10 to 15 potatoes)
1¼ pounds fresh salmon fillet, without skin or bones
3 tablespoons capers, drained
3 tablespoons cilantro, chopped
6 cloves garlic, minced
3 tablespoons fresh lime juice
1½ teaspoons salt
1½ teaspoons cayenne pepper
1 small egg, beaten
3 tablespoons vegetable oil
Lemon slices for garnish

Salsa

3 ears of corn
2 tablespoons olive oil
2 medium tomatoes
½ small red onion
3 tablespoons cilantro, chopped
3 tablespoons fresh lime juice
1 teaspoon garlic, minced
2 teaspoons sesame oil
½ teaspoon salt
½ teaspoon ground black pepper

For the salmon cakes

1. Cook potatoes with the skins on, drain and cool.
2. Cut salmon into chunks and chop in a food processor to a fine consistency.
3. Combine salmon in a bowl with the capers, cilantro, garlic, lime juice, salt, and cayenne pepper.
4. When potatoes are cool enough to handle, remove skins, and grate in food processor or by hand. Add the potatoes to the salmon mixture.
5. Add beaten egg and combine gently.
6. With your hands, form the mixture into 12 cakes. Refrigerate for at least 20 minutes.

For the salsa

1. Preheat grill to highest temperature.
2. Rub the corn kernels with olive oil.
3. Place on grill and toast for about 8 minutes, turning occasionally to brown evenly.
4. When cool enough to handle, remove kernels with a sharp knife.
5. Mix the corn with the remaining salsa ingredients and set aside.

To finish the salmon cakes

1. Heat the oil in a skillet and fry the salmon cakes for 3 to 4 minutes on each side until golden brown in color. Be careful not to let the heat get too high or they may brown too quickly.
2. Drain on paper towels and serve immediately with the corn salsa and slices of lemon for garnish.

GARLIC & HERB CRUSTED PORK TENDERLOIN
Gilroy Garlic Festival

Third Place Winner: Jamie Miller of Maple Grove, Minnesota
Pork tenderloin has become very popular because of its leanness and appealing taste. Here the tenderloin has a delicious garlic crust created with "fresh" (soft) bread crumbs, made by simply placing pieces of untoasted bread in a food processor and chopping to desired texture.

Serves 6

Roasted Garlic
1 large head garlic
1 tablespoon olive oil

Pork
2 cups fresh bread crumbs from crustless French bread
$^1/_4$ cup chopped fresh parsley
3 cloves garlic, minced
$^3/_4$ tablespoon fresh rosemary, minced
$^1/_2$ teaspoon bay leaves, finely crumbled
1 pork tenderloin, about $^3/_4$ pound
Salt and pepper
1 large egg, beaten
2 tablespoons butter
1 tablespoon olive oil

Preheat oven to 375 degrees

1. To roast garlic: peel papery skin from outside of garlic head. Slice off top to expose cloves. Drizzle with 1 tablespoon olive oil. Wrap in foil and bake 45 minutes.

2. When cool enough to handle, squeeze garlic into a small bowl and mash with fork to form a smooth paste.

3. Meanwhile, combine bread crumbs and next 4 ingredients and mix well.

4. Sprinkle pork with salt and pepper.

5. Dip pork into egg, then into bread crumb mixture.

6. Melt butter and oil in a large ovenproof, nonstick skillet over medium-high heat. Add pork and brown on all sides.

7. Place skillet in oven and roast pork until thermometer inserted into center registers 150 to 155 degrees, about 15 to 20 minutes.

8. Transfer pork to cutting board and let rest 5 minutes.

9. Slice on the diagonal and serve.

LOBSTER WRAPS
Maine Lobster Festival

Here's an ingenious way to serve some succulent lobster meat for a luncheon or picnic. It earned Jessica Yankura of Rockland, Maine, first prize at the recipe contest at the Maine Lobster Festival.

Serves 4

2 cups cooked lobster meat
8 ounces grated Muenster cheese
8 cilantro sprigs
4 tortillas
Fresh lime juice, to taste
Salsa

1. Cut the cooked lobster meat into chunks. Divide lobster meat and cheese evenly over tortillas and place 2 sprigs of fresh cilantro onto each tortilla. Sprinkle with lime juice and roll the filled tortilla.

2. Wrap the filled tortilla in aluminum foil and warm on a grill or in a microwave oven. Serve lobster wraps with salsa.

BOUILLABAISSE À LA MAINE
Maine Lobster Festival

Dennis Delpape of East Orland, Maine, won second prize at the Maine Lobster Festival with this aromatic bouillabaisse (fish stew), which brings together a striking collection of seafood.

Serves 4

3 cups white wine
1 yellow onion, peeled and sliced thin
$^1/_2$ pound haddock, cut into $^3/_4$-inch pieces
$^1/_4$ pound small scallops
$^1/_2$ pound clams in shells
$^1/_2$ pound mussels in shells
$^1/_2$ pound crabmeat
2 small lobsters
2 lobster heads
4 cloves garlic, peeled and minced
2 green onions, trimmed and coarsely chopped
4 small white potatoes, peeled and cut into bite-sized cubes
3 tablespoons olive oil
8 sprigs thyme
2 sprigs rosemary
2 sprigs tarragon
4 sage leaves
4 sprigs parsley
6 basil leaves
2 cups fish stock
2 tomatoes, skinned and diced
4 lettuce tops (for serving)

1. Bring wine and onion to a simmer in a saucepan.
2. Add haddock and scallops. Cover and steam gently until cooked through, approximately 3–5 minutes. With a slotted spoon, remove seafood and hold on a plate. Reserve the cooking liquid.

3. In a heavy-bottomed soup pot, sauté the garlic, green onions, and potatoes in olive oil until green onions are translucent, 4–5 minutes. Add reserved cooking liquid, whole lobsters, lobster heads, and tomato. Simmer over a medium heat for 10 minutes. *Note: you may want to break apart the whole lobsters just prior to cooking.*

4. Finely chop all the herbs and add to soup pot along with fish stock, clams, mussels, and crabmeat. Add the cooked haddock and scallops. Stir, cover, and allow to simmer for 5 minutes. (Make sure the mussels have opened.)

5. Place the lettuce tops in the bottom of 4 serving bowls. Ladle the stew on top of the lettuce and serve.

SPAGHETTINI WITH LOBSTER SAUCE
Maine Lobster Festival

Ann Dean of South Thomaston, Maine, placed third in the Maine Lobster Cook-off with this unique recipe in which lobster is cooked in a tomato sauce. When buying lobsters, look for ones that are recently caught and still feisty. It's best to cook them the same day they are purchased.

Serves 3

2 tablespoons olive oil
6 garlic cloves, peeled
Two 28-ounce cans whole, peeled tomatoes
2 tablespoons chopped flatleaf parsley
2 tablespoons chopped fresh oregano
1 bay leaf
2 peppercorns
3 Maine lobsters
1 pound spaghettini
Grated Romano cheese

1. In a pot large enough to hold the lobsters, warm olive oil and crush the garlic through a garlic press into the oil, stirring (do not let garlic brown).

2. With your hands, crush tomatoes into pot. Bring sauce to a simmer. Once simmering, add parsley, oregano, bay leaf, and peppercorns to sauce and stir. Add live lobsters, cover pot, and cook over medium-high heat until lobsters are red, about 12–15 minutes.

3. While lobsters are cooking, bring a large pot of salted water to a boil and cook spaghettini. Drain. Place lobsters over spaghettini and pour sauce over lobsters and pasta. Sprinkle with Romano cheese and serve.

BIG BOB GIBSON'S BARBECUED PORK SHOULDER

Memphis in May World Championship Barbecue Cooking Contest

Big Bob Gibson's is the name of both a barbecue team and two landmark restaurants in Decatur, Alabama. Don McLemore (see photo on next page), the grandson of Big Bob, still runs the 75-year old family restaurant and competes on the team which took the prestigious 2000 Memphis in May Grand Championship Prize with this recipe.

---

1 pork shoulder or pork butt
(note: a pork butt is usually half the size of a shoulder)

Big Bob Gibson's Championship Red Sauce or your favorite barbecue sauce

Big Bob Gibson's Bar-B-Q Pork Injection
1 cup apple cider vinegar
1 cup soy sauce
1 cup sugar
$^2/_3$ cup salt
$^1/_2$ cup water
$^1/_4$ cup vegetable oil
3 tablespoons Worcestershire sauce
1 teaspoon cayenne pepper
1 teaspoon black pepper

Big Bob Gibson's Bar-B-Q All Purpose Rub
1 cup dark brown sugar
$^1/_2$ cup garlic salt
$^1/_3$ cup onion salt
$^1/_2$ cup paprika
2 tablespoons chili powder
1 $^1/_2$ teaspoon oregano leaves
1 tablespoon cayenne pepper
1 teaspoon ground cumin
1 teaspoon black pepper

Preheat grill to 225 degrees for slow, indirect cooking.

1. Mix together all marinade ingredients until well incorporated.

2. Using a meat syringe, inject the marinade into the meat approximately every inch. Try to rotate the syringe as the marinade goes in to avoid creating pockets of fluid.

3. Apply the rub liberally all over the meat and rub in so it adheres to the meat.

4. Allow the meat to sit in refrigerator for two hours.

5. Place on grill and cook approximately one hour per pound until the internal temperature is 195 degrees. During the last 20–30 minutes of cooking, baste frequently with the barbecue sauce.

6. Remove the meat from grill and pull the meat apart. Serve in sandwiches with coleslaw.

Note: If you do not have a meat syringe, then place the seasoned meat and marinade in a ziploc bag and proceed to step 4.

BIG BOB GIBSON'S BAKED BEANS
Memphis in May World Championship Barbecue Cooking Contest

Big Bob Gibson's restaurants in Decatur draw barbecue aficionados from all over the world. Chris Lilly graciously showed us the way to cook baked beans just as they are served at the restaurants.

Serves 20

10 cups of canned baked kidney beans
1 cup diced bell pepper
1 cup diced onions
¹/₂ cup Worcestershire sauce
¹/₂ cup Big Bob Gibson Championship Red Sauce, or ketchup
¹/₂ cup brown sugar
2 tablespoons mustard

Preheat oven to 350 degrees

1. Combine all ingredients in a large shallow baking dish and mix well.

2. Bake uncovered for 45 minutes at 350 degrees.

3. Stir and cook an additional 30 minutes.

BIG BOB GIBSON'S COLESLAW

Memphis in May World Championship Barbecue Cooking Contest

Barbecued pork shoulder is traditionally served piled high on sandwiches with lots of coleslaw. To save time, use a food processor to shred the cabbage.

Serves 20

2 large heads of green cabbage
1$\frac{1}{4}$ cups sugar
1$\frac{1}{4}$ cups distilled vinegar
2 tablespoons salt

1. Core and grate the cabbage in a food processor or with a hand grater.
2. Place the vinegar, sugar, and salt together in a large bowl and mix well. Pour over the cabbage and allow to sit in the refrigerator for at least several hours.
3. Serve chilled.

Note: For more information about Big Bob Gibson's, check out their web site at **www.bigbobgibsonbbq.com**

GRILLED COOK-OFF CABBAGE

Memphis in May World Championship Barbecue Cooking Contest

Serves 4

1 head of cabbage
1 Vidalia or other sweet onion
4 tablespoons butter or margarine, softened
$^1/_2$ teaspoon seasoning salt (or to taste)
$^1/_4$ teaspoon black pepper (or to taste)

Preheat grill for cooking over a low, indirect fire (250 degrees for a gas grill)

1. Remove core from the cabbage and cut cabbage into quarters. Place on a sheet of aluminum foil which is large enough to completely wrap the cabbage. Sprinkle seasoning salt and pepper over the cabbage pieces.

2. Rub one tablespoon of butter over each quarter.

3. Slice onion into four thick slices and place one slice on top of each cabbage quarter. Wrap cabbage in foil.

4. Place on grill for approximately two hours. Carefully open aluminum foil to avoid steam burns. Serve warm.

MUSTARD GLAZED MUSCOVY DUCK BREAST WITH SWEET ONION AND CUCUMBER KIM CHEE

Napa Valley Mustard Festival

Peter Pahk, Executive Chef, Silverado Country Club, Napa California
The Napa Valley Mustard Festival attracts the top chefs from the region,
who compete for the "Best Chef of the Year" award.

Serves 6

6 seedless cucumbers, peeled, halved, and cut lengthwise into ¼-inch slices
Kosher salt and freshly ground black pepper, to taste
6 Muscovy duck hen breasts
6 ounces hot sweet mustard
1 Maui (or other sweet) onion, julienned
¼ cup rice vinegar
¼ cup fish sauce
2 tablespoons peeled and finely julienned fresh ginger
3 cloves garlic, peeled and sliced paper thin
2 tablespoons sugar
Roasted black and white sesame seeds, for garnish

1. Place cucumber slices in a colander with a generous sprinkling of kosher salt, toss, and let drain for 20–25 minutes.

2. Trim duck breasts of excess fat and score skin in a cross-hatch fashion. Season with salt and pepper.

3. Warm a skillet large enough to hold duck breasts over a medium-low heat. Place duck skin side down in skillet. Spoon enough mustard over tops to coat. Render breasts until no fat remains and skin is crisp.

4. Turn duck breasts over and brush skin side with mustard. Cook another 2 minutes. Turn again and repeat process quickly just so mustard is caramelized on both sides of breasts. Remove from skillet and reserve.

5. Pat dry cucumber slices and combine with rest of ingredients (except sesame seeds) in a bowl. This is kim chee.

6. Cut duck breast on the bias. Fan slices onto 6 plates and surround with a portion of the kim chee. Garnish with sesame seeds.

FRESH SONOMA LAMB ACHIOTE WITH SMOKED ONION MUSTARD SAUCE

Napa Valley Mustard Festival

This recipe comes from executive chef Patrick Finney and sous chef Kelly MacDonald of the Napa Valley Wine Train, one of Napa's hot culinary destinations. Every year they develop recipes like this one to enter in the Mustard recipe competition. Achiote paste can be found in Mexican or Latin-American grocery stores.

Serves 4

2 racks lamb, trimmed of all fat and silver skin
2 ounces achiote chili paste

Smoked Onion Mustard Sauce
2 cups demi-glace
1 1/2 cups cabernet sauvignon
2 teaspoons tumeric
1 teaspoon ground coriander seeds
1 tablespoon black pepper
1 teaspoon kosher salt
4 tablespoons butter
1 1/2 cups country-style Dijon mustard
2 tablespoons honey
1 large onion, smoked and finely chopped

Preheat grill

1. Light the grill, using mesquite charcoal.

2. Season lamb with salt and pepper. Rub achiote paste onto meat.

3. Place lamb on grill over direct heat and cook for 15 minutes.

4. Remove lamb to indirect heat and cook for about 30 minutes (for medium-rare), or until lamb reaches an internal temperature of 110 to 115 degrees. Remove from grill and allow to rest for 10 minutes.

5. To make sauce: Bring demi-glace and wine to a boil in a small saucepan. Lower heat and simmer for 10 minutes.

6. Add spices and salt to the demi-glace mixture and simmer an additional 10 minutes.

7. Whisk in butter, mustard, honey, and chopped onion, stirring, until butter is melted and incorporated into sauce (do not allow sauce to come to a boil once the mustard is added, as it will make the sauce bitter). Immediately remove from heat.

8. Place a pool of sauce on the plate and arrange lamb chops on top. Serve.

* *If you don't want to make demi-glace the traditional way, here's a short cut for the home cook. Bring two cups of beef bouillon to a boil. Combine 1 tablespoon of cornstarch with 3 tablespoons of cold water and stir until the cornstarch is dissolved. While the bouillon is simmering (not boiling), slowly add the cornstarch mixture, stirring constantly. The bouillon will start to thicken. When it can coat the back of a spoon, it is finished and can be used as demi-glace.*

** *To smoke onions: Spread a layer of applewood chips that have been soaked in cold water over a bed of hot coals. Place onions on grill, cover, and cook slowly for one hour. Finish in a 350-degree oven until onions are very soft.*

SKEWERED MANGO SHRIMP WITH PINEAPPLE RUM SALSA

Newman's Own / Good Housekeeping Recipe Contest

1999 Runner Up, Multi-Product Category: Jeri Dunlop, The Woodlands, Texas
Inspired by the flavors of *Newman's Own Pineapple Salsa,* Jeri took the
taste of the islands one step further with the addition of rum and mango.

Serves 4 as a main dish

8 bamboo skewers, soaked in water for 30 minutes
24 large shrimp (about 1 pound), shelled and deveined
1 ripe mango, peeled and cut into 1-inch pieces
1 large red bell pepper, cored and cut into 1-inch pieces
4 green onions, cut into 1¹/₂-inch pieces
¹/₃ cup Newman's Own Family Recipe Italian Dressing
1 jar (16 ounces) Newman's Own Pineapple Salsa
2 tablespoons dark rum
3 cups hot cooked rice

1. On skewers, alternately thread shrimp, mango, red pepper, and green onions. Place skewers in a 13 x 9-inch glass baking dish and pour *Newman's Own Family Recipe Italian Dressing* and *Newman's Own Pineapple Salsa* over skewers, coating evenly. Marinate for 15 minutes at room temperature or for 1 hour in the refrigerator.

2. Preheat the broiler. Remove skewers from marinade and place on rack in boiler pan. Reserve marinade. With broiler pan at the closest position to source of heat, broil the skewers for 4 minutes per side, or just until shrimp turns opaque.

3. Remove skewers to plate; keep warm. Pour salsa marinade into a 2-quart saucepan and heat to boiling over high heat. Boil marinade for 3 minutes. Add rum and boil 1 minute longer.

4. To serve, place 2 skewers of shrimp over rice on a plate, then top with some of the cooked salsa mixture.

SENSATIONAL STUFFED SOCKAROONI PORTOBELLOS

Newman's Own / Good Housekeeping Recipe Contest

1999 Runner Up, Pasta Sauce Category: Phyllis Kapiloff, Stamford, Connecticut.

In a quest for simple, tasty, healthy food, Phyllis developed this recipe using fresh flavors from the garden and pantry. Omit sausage for a terrific vegetarian dish.

Serves 6 as a main dish

1 medium eggplant (about 1¹/₄ pounds)
1 large Spanish onion, chopped
2 cloves garlic, peeled and minced
¹/₄ cup olive oil
12 ounces sweet chicken sausage (optional)
¹/₂ cup freshly grated Parmesan cheese
¹/₂ cup red wine
1 jar (26 ounces) Newman's Own Sockarooni Sauce
6 large portobello mushroom caps (about 4 ounces each)

Preheat oven to 400 degrees

1. Pierce eggplant with a fork in several places. Place on a foil-lined cookie sheet and bake for 45 minutes, or until soft. Remove from oven and let cool. Keep oven on.

2. While eggplant is baking, sauté onion and garlic over medium heat in 2 tablespoons of the olive oil, in a 12-inch nonstick skillet, until translucent, about 15 minutes (do not let onions brown). Set aside in a large bowl.

3. Remove casing from sausage and coarsely chop sausage. In the same 12-inch skillet as used for onion mixture, sauté sausage until thoroughly cooked, about 12 minutes. Add sausage to onion mixture.

(continued)

4. When cool enough to handle, slit eggplant and scoop out pulp and mash. Stir egg-plant and ¼ cup of the Parmesan cheese into onion mixture.

5. In a 2-quart saucepan, heat red wine to boiling over medium-high heat and simmer for 4 minutes. Stir in *Newman's Own Sockarooni Sauce* and remove from heat.

6. In a 15½-inch by 10½-inch jelly roll pan, place mushroom caps, rounded side up. Brush mushrooms with remaining 2 tablespoons of olive oil and bake for 10 minutes. Turn mushrooms and spoon 2 tablespoons of the sauce into each mushroom. Top with ½ cup eggplant mixture, followed by 2 more tablespoons of the sauce. Sprinkle remaining cheese over mushrooms and return to oven. Bake for 15 minutes and serve immediately with remaining sauce.

A DROWNING POOL OF PRALINE IN A CHOCOLATE TART

Newman's Own / Good Housekeeping Recipe Contest

1998 Grand Prize Winner, Chocolate Category: Kaija Keel, Los Angeles, California

A professional artist who teaches at a local grammar school, Kaija created this heavenly dessert by combining her own creativity with recipes handed down to her by her grandmother.

Serves 24

Tart Shell
$^3/_4$ *cup butter ($1^1/_2$ sticks), softened*
$1^1/_2$ *cups all-purpose flour*
$^1/_3$ *cup confectioners' sugar*

Praline-Chocolate Filling
2 bars (3 ounces each) Newman's Own Organics Chocolate *(Sweet Dark Chocolate or Sweet Dark Chocolate with Orange Oil), broken into pieces*
$^3/_4$ *cup heavy or whipping cream*
1 bag (9 $^1/_2$ ounces) caramels, unwrapped
$1^1/_2$ *cups pecans, toasted and coarsely chopped*

(continued)

Preheat oven to 375 degrees

To Prepare Tart Shell

1. Pulse together all of the tart shell ingredients in a food processor until they form moist crumbs. Sprinkle crumbs in a 9-inch tart pan with removable bottom and press crumbs together to form a crust on bottom and up sides. Prick dough all over with a fork. Line tart shell with aluminum foil and fill with pie weights, dried beans, or uncooked rice. Bake for 25 minutes, remove foil and weights, and bake for another 15–20 minutes until golden, pressing crust with the back of a spoon if it puffs, and loosely covering dark spots with aluminum foil. Remove from oven and allow to cool on a rack.

To Prepare Praline-Chocolate Filling

1. Combine chocolate and $\frac{1}{4}$ cup of the cream in a 1-quart saucepan. Melt, stirring frequently, over medium-low heat. Pour chocolate mixture, reserving 2 tablespoons, in bottom of cooled crust, spreading evenly. Chill tart shell, as well as reserved 2 tablespoons of chocolate mixture.

2. In a 2-quart saucepan, over medium-low heat, heat caramels and remaining $\frac{1}{2}$ cup of cream until melted and smooth, stirring occasionally. Stir in pecans and quickly pour over chocolate layer, spreading evenly.

3. In a 1-quart saucepan, over low heat, heat reserved chocolate mixture for 1 to 2 minutes, stirring until melted, or microwave for 10 seconds. Using a fork, drizzle melted chocolate in a zigzag pattern over the top of the tart. Chill at least 1 hour and keep tart stored in the refrigerator.

STEAK KABOBS
Riverside Orange Blossom Festival

First Place Winner, Salads and Appetizers Category: Annette Vigil, Riverside, California. Reprinted from the *Riverside Orange Blossom Cookbook 2000*. Asian satés—meats grilled on skewers—have worked their way into American cuisine and make a wonderful addition to any outdoor party.

Makes approximately 16 appetizers

Sixteen 6- to 8-inch bamboo skewers
1 cup orange juice
One 6-ounce can crushed pineapple
$^1/_2$ cup honey
$^1/_2$ cup brown sugar
4 cloves garlic, peeled and minced
One $1^1/_2$- to 2-pound flank steak, cut thinly against the grain into approximately 16 slices

1. Soak bamboo skewers in cold water for at least 30 minutes.

2. Mix together orange juice, pineapple, honey, brown sugar, and garlic. Thread a slice of flank steak onto bamboo skewers and place in container large enough to hold skewers. Pour marinade over meat, covering. Marinate for 1 hour.

3. Start fire or turn on grill. Grill skewers over low coals for about 10 minutes, turn, and cook another 10 minutes.

ORANGE AND ARUGULA SALAD WITH FENNEL AND PEPPER-CRUSTED SALMON

Riverside Orange Blossom Festival

Grand Prize Winner, Salads and Appetizers Category: Claudia Crager, Moreno Valley, California. Reprinted from the *Riverside Orange Blossom Cookbook 2000*. Fennel-flavored salmon atop a colorful and piquant arugula salad makes this a wonderful combination. Try grilling the salmon for extra flavor.

Serves 4

2 navel oranges
1 tablespoon fennel seed
1 tablespoon black peppercorns
4 salmon fillets, about 4 ounces each
1 teaspoon salt, or to taste
2 cups baby arugula, washed and drained well
1 fennel bulb, cut into very thin strips
$^1/_2$ cup roasted red bell pepper, cut into thin strips
$^1/_4$ cup whole Niçoise olives, pitted
1 tablespoon fresh lemon juice
2 tablespoons extra-virgin olive oil, or to taste
2 tablespoons chopped fresh basil leaves
1 tablespoon balsamic vinegar

1. Using a sharp knife, cut off the orange tops and cut away the outside skin to expose the flesh of each orange. Use a paring knife to cut in between the membranes, removing the sections. Place orange sections in a medium bowl and set aside.

(continued)

2. Crush the fennel and peppercorn seeds using a mortar and pestle or spice grinder. (If desired and time permits, toast seeds before grinding them.) Season the top of the salmon fillets with salt and sprinkle fennel-peppercorn mixture over each fillet, pressing the seasonings into the fish with your fingertips.

3. Preheat the oven to 400 degrees. Heat a large, nonstick sauté pan over medium-high heat. When hot, add the fillets, spice side down. Sear the salmon until the fillet edges have begun to crisp slightly and the spice aroma is very apparent, about 5 minutes. Transfer the salmon, spice side up, into an ovenproof dish and place into the oven. Bake for 8 to 10 minutes, or until the fish is completely cooked and firm. The fillets should flake easily if tested with a fork.

4. While the salmon bakes, add arugula, fennel, red bell pepper, olives, lemon juice, olive oil, basil, and vinegar to bowl with orange sections. Toss well and adjust seasonings, as desired.

5. Remove salmon from oven. With a slotted spoon, divide the orange salad mixture evenly onto individual serving plates and top with a piece of salmon, spice side up, reserving salad dressing. Drizzle any remaining salad dressing over the salmon and serve.

SUNSHINE CHEESECAKE
Riverside Orange Blossom Festival

First Place Winner, Desserts Category: Dayle S. Sims, Moreno Valley, California.

Orange slices adorn the top of this beautiful cheesecake, which gets an extra boost of flavor from white chocolate and a gingersnap cookie crust. Remember it needs to chill overnight before serving.

Makes 1 cheesecake

Crust
One 8-ounce bag gingersnap cookies, ground (about 3 cups)
6 tablespoons (³/₄ stick) butter, melted
1¹/₂ teaspoons minced fresh orange peel

Filling
1¹/₂ cups fresh orange juice
One 3-inch piece unpeeled fresh ginger, thinly sliced
Four 8-ounce packages cream cheese, at room temperature
²/₃ cup sugar
1 tablespoon minced fresh orange peel
1 tablespoon vanilla extract
8 ounces white chocolate, melted
4 large eggs

Oranges
4 cups water
2 cups sugar
3 seedless, unpeeled oranges, cut into paper-thin slices
Fresh mint leaves, for garnish

(continued)

To Make Crust

1. Stir together crust ingredients in a medium bowl until gingersnap crumbs are moist. Press crumbs on the bottom and up 2 inches of the sides of a 9 x 2 ³/₄-inch springform pan. Set aside.

To Make Filling

Preheat oven to 350 degrees

1. Boil orange juice and ginger in a heavy saucepan until reduced to 3 tablespoons, about 12 minutes.

2. Using an electric mixer, beat together the cream cheese, sugar, orange peel, and vanilla in a large bowl until smooth.

3. Strain reduced orange juice mixture and add to bowl with cream cheese. With mixer running, add white chocolate and beat until all ingredients are combined. Reduce mixer to a low speed, adding eggs one at a time, until just combined.

4. Pour batter into crust and bake until the top is dry and sides puff slightly, about 50 minutes. Transfer cheesecake to a rack and cool. Once cool, cover and refrigerate overnight.

To Make Oranges

1. Cover a large rack with waxed paper.

2. Combine water and sugar in a heavy, shallow pot and stir over medium heat until sugar dissolves, about 5 minutes.

3. Add orange slices, one at a time, to water and sugar mixture, adjusting heat so that syrup bubbles only around the edge of the pot. Cook oranges this way for 1 hour.

4. Turn over top layer of oranges and continue cooking until oranges are translucent and orange peels are tender, about 1 hour longer.

5. Arrange orange slices in a single layer on prepared rack, reserving sugar syrup. Dry 1 hour.

6. Boil sugar syrup until thick, about 6 minutes.

To Assemble Cheesecake

Run a small knife around edge of cheesecake, loosening from pan. Remove to a cake plate. Overlap orange slices atop cheesecake. Reheat orange syrup, if necessary, and brush over orange slices. Garnish with mint and serve.

LEMON SCENTED SABLE COOKIES
Beaver Creek National Pastry Championship

Normally, we get recipes directly from the competitions. However, with the complexity of the entries at Beaver Creek, we created some pastries especially for home cooks. The recipes come from our host, Marcel Desaulniers, chef/owner of the world famous Trellis Restaurant in Williamsburg, Virginia.

Makes 24 cookies

2 cups all-purpose flour, sifted
6 ounces unsalted butter, cut into $^{1}/_{2}$-ounce pieces
$^{2}/_{3}$ cup granulated sugar
2 teaspoons fresh lemon zest
2 large egg yolks
1 teaspoon vanilla extract

Preheat the oven to 350 degrees

1. Combine the butter, sugar, and lemon zest in the bowl of an electric mixer fitted with a paddle. Mix on low speed for 1 minute. Increase the speed to medium and beat for 4 minutes until soft, scraping down the sides of the bowl as necessary.

2. Add the egg yolks 1 at a time, allowing one to fully incorporate before adding the other.

3. Add the vanilla extract and mix on medium speed for 1 minute.

4. Turn the mixer to low speed; gradually add the sifted flour until combined.

5. Place the dough onto a large piece of wax paper and form it into a cylinder measuring about 2 inches in diameter. Refrigerate the dough for at least 1 hour.

6. Remove the dough from the refrigerator. After removing the wax paper, use a sharp knife to slice $^{1}/_{2}$-inch thick disks from the cylinder.

7. Place the cookies onto a nonstick baking sheet and bake in the preheated oven until lightly golden brown, about 12 minutes. Remove the cookies from the oven and allow to cool on the tray for about 5 minutes.

PISTACHIO ICE CREAM
Beaver Creek National Pastry Championship

With the availability of low-cost ice cream freezers, there is no excuse for depriving yourself of the luxurious taste of homemade ice cream.

Makes 1 quart

$^3/_4$ cup shelled pistachio nuts, chopped medium fine
$1^1/_2$ cups heavy cream
$1^1/_2$ cups half-and-half
$^3/_4$ cup granulated sugar
4 large egg yolks
2 teaspoons pure vanilla extract

1. Bring to a boil the heavy cream, $1^1/_2$ cups half-and-half, and $^1/_2$ cup granulated sugar in a medium saucepan over medium-high heat. When hot, stir to dissolve the sugar.

2. While the cream mixture is heating, place egg yolks and $^1/_4$ cup granulated sugar in the bowl of an electric mixer fitted with a paddle. Beat on high speed for 4 minutes until slightly thickened and pale yellow, occasionally scraping down the sides of the bowl. *Note: if the cream mixture has not yet started to boil, adjust the mixer speed to low and continue to mix until you are ready for step 3.*

3. Gradually pour the boiling cream mixture into the beaten egg yolk and sugar mixture and mix on medium to combine, about 1 minute.

4. Return the combined mixture to the saucepan and place over medium heat, stirring constantly. Bring to a temperature of 185 degrees (about 3 minutes).

5. Place mixture in a stainless steel bowl. Cool in an ice-water bath to a temperature of 40 to 45 degrees. Add the vanilla extract and stir to incorporate.

6. Freeze in an ice-cream freezer following the manufacturer's instructions.

7. Transfer the semifrozen ice cream to a plastic container. Add the chopped pistachios and use a rubber spatula to fold until well combined.

8. Securely cover the container, then place in the freezer for several hours before serving.

CHOCOLATE TRUFFLES

Beaver Creek National Pastry Championship

It's surprising how easy it is to make beautiful and delicious truffles. This recipe gives three options for garnishes, but feel free to use your own ideas.

Makes 24 truffles

8 ounces semisweet chocolate, coarsely chopped
1 cup heavy cream
1 tablespoon granulated sugar
$^1/_4$ cup shelled pistachio nuts, chopped fine
$^1/_4$ cup cocoa powder
$^1/_4$ cup confectioners' sugar

1. Place chopped semisweet chocolate in a medium bowl.
2. Heat heavy cream and granulated sugar in a small saucepan over medium heat. When hot, stir to dissolve the sugar. Bring to a boil.
3. Pour the boiling cream over the chopped chocolate. Set aside for 5 minutes before stirring with a whisk until smooth.
4. To chill, pour the mixture (called ganache) onto a pan (approximately 9 x 9-inch) pan with sides and use a rubber spatula to spread the ganache in a smooth, even layer. Place the ganache in the freezer for 15 minutes, or in the refrigerator for 30 minutes, until very firm to the touch.
5. Place each of the three garnishes—chopped pistachios, cocoa powder, confectioners' sugar—on its own separate, medium sized plate. Set aside. Remove the firm ganache from the freezer or the refrigerator. Making 24 portions, roll each one in your palms in a gentle circular motion, using just enough pressure to form smooth, round truffles.
6. Roll each truffle through one of the three garnishes (see step 5) and refrigerate the truffles on a clean, large dinner plate until needed.

ROSEMARY-GARLIC PORK TENDERLOIN WRAPPED IN PANCETTA

Stonewall Peach Jamboree

From *Weber's Art of the Grill* (Chronicle Books). Pork tenderloin has become a favorite among chefs who appreciate its versatility and leanness. Pancetta, a cured (not smoked) Italian bacon, can be found in Italian specialty stores. This is delicious served with the Honey-Ginger Peach Sauce.

Serves 6

3 garlic cloves, minced
2 sprigs fresh rosemary, leaves removed from stem and chopped
¼ teaspoon freshly ground pepper
3 pork tenderloins, about 1 pound each
1 egg white beaten with 1 tablespoon of water
¼ pound thinly sliced pancetta

1. In a small bowl, combine the garlic, rosemary, and pepper. Rub mixture over the pork tenderloins, pressing it into the meat. Brush tenderloins liberally with the egg white mixture. Wrap each tenderloin with slices of the pancetta. Secure pancetta with toothpicks or kitchen string.

2. Grill tenderloins over a medium, direct heat until browned on all sides, about 2 minutes per side. Move to the side of the grill and cook over an indirect heat for 15 to 20 minutes longer, or until center is barely pink and internal temperature is 155 degrees. Remove from heat, cover, and allow to rest for 5 to 10 minutes. Slice and serve warm.

HONEY-GINGER PEACH SAUCE

Stonewall Peach Jamboree

From *Weber's Art of the Grill* (Chronicle Books). This is a great sauce to use for outdoor grilling of meats and poultry; like any typical barbecue sauce, brush it on during the last 10 minutes of grilling time.

Makes 8 servings

4 medium peaches, peeled and pitted
2 tablespoons honey
2 tablespoons lemon juice
1^1/$_2$ teaspoons minced ginger
1 teaspoon balsamic vinegar
5 drops hot pepper sauce

1. Cut 3 of the peaches into chunks. Place in a food processor or blender along with honey, lemon juice, ginger, vinegar, and hot pepper sauce. Process until smooth.

2. Pour peach mixture into a small saucepan and bring to a boil. Reduce to a simmer and cook, uncovered and stirring, for 15 minutes or until slightly thickened.

3. Finely chop remaining peach and stir into sauce.

PEACH CREAM KUCHEN
Stonewall Peach Jamboree

A "kuchen" is a cheese- or fruit-filled cake which originated in Germany and was commonly served for breakfast.

Serves 6 to 8

2 cups sifted flour
$^3/_4$ cup sugar
$^1/_4$ teaspoon baking powder
1 teaspoon salt
$^1/_2$ cup butter or margarine
2–3 fresh peaches (or one 28-ounce can of peach slices)
1 teaspoon cinnamon
2 egg yolks
1 cup sour cream

Preheat oven to 400 degrees

1. Lightly grease a 9 x 9 x 2-inch baking pan.
2. Sift together the flour, $^1/_4$ cup sugar, baking powder, and salt into a mixing bowl.
3. Cut in the butter with a pastry blender until the mixture resembles fine crumbs.
   Note: you can also do this in a food processor; be sure to use the "pulse" control.
4. Transfer mixture to the baking pan and press crumbs firmly against bottom and sides.
5. Peel and slice the peaches about $^1/_4$-inch thick. If using canned peaches, drain them thoroughly. Reserve some slices for a garnish.
6. Layer the peaches evenly over the crust in the pan.
7. Stir together $^1/_2$ cup sugar and cinnamon until well combined. Sprinkle over the fruit.
8. Bake in the preheated oven for 15 minutes.
9. Beat together the egg yolks and sour cream. Spoon over the partially baked kuchen and continue baking for 20 minutes or until golden brown.
10. Use any remaining peach slices to garnish the top of the cake. Serve warm or thoroughly chilled.

PEACHY-PINEAPPLE SMOOTHIE

Stonewall Peach Jamboree

Peaches and pineapple make a terrific combination in this delicious creamy smoothie.

Serves 4 to 6

28 ounces of sliced peaches, fresh or canned
$^1/_2$ cup chilled pineapple juice
$^1/_2$ cup sugar
1 pint vanilla ice cream, softened

Process first three ingredients in a blender until smooth, stopping once to scrape down sides. Add ice cream and process until smooth. Serve.

HONEY CRUNCH PECAN PIE
National Pie Championship

2000 Best of Show and First Place, Nut Category: Sarah Spaugh, Winston-Salem, North Carolina
This grand-prize-winning pie has a rich double whammy of pecans, plus a special touch from the bourbon and honey.

Makes one 9-inch pie

Crust
2 cups flour
1 teaspoon salt
¼ cup hydrogenated shortening
6 tablespoons cold water
1 teaspoon white or apple cider vinegar

Filling
4 eggs, lightly beaten
¼ cup firmly packed brown sugar
¼ cup granulated sugar
½ teaspoon salt
1 cup light corn syrup
2 tablespoons butter, melted
1 teaspoon vanilla
1 tablespoon bourbon (optional)
1 cup chopped pecans

Topping
⅓ cup firmly packed brown sugar
3 tablespoons butter or margarine
3 tablespoons honey
1½ cups pecan halves

(continued)

131

To Make Crust

1. Combine flour, salt, and shortening in a large bowl. Gradually mix in water and vinegar. Cut together ingredients until dough will hold together. Press dough into a ball and lightly flour. Wrap in plastic wrap and chill for 20 minutes.

2. Roll chilled dough between pieces of waxed paper into a circle about $\frac{1}{8}$-inch thick and press into a 9-inch pie pan. Cover and refrigerate.

To Make Filling

1. Preheat oven to 350 degrees. Combine all filling ingredients in a large bowl and mix well. Spoon into unbaked pie crust and bake for 15 minutes. Remove from oven, cover the edge of crust with aluminum foil, and return to oven, baking for another 20 minutes.

To Make Topping

1. While pie is baking, combine sugar, butter, and honey in a medium saucepan. Cook over medium heat, stirring, until sugar dissolves, about 2 minutes. Add nuts and stir just to coat.

2. Remove pie from oven and spoon topping evenly over pie. Return to oven and bake for another 10 to 20 minutes, or until topping is bubbly and golden brown. Allow pie to cool to room temperature before serving.

BERRY RHUBARB PIE
National Pie Championship

First Place, Fruit and Berry Category: Susan Gills, Boulder, Colorado
If you have not tried it before, the combination of rhubarb and berries makes for a truly outstanding pie.

Makes one 10-inch pie

Filling
1 cup blackberries
1 cup raspberries
2 cups rhubarb, cut into $^1/_2$-inch pieces
$^3/_4$ cup sugar
$^1/_4$ cup flour
1 tablespoon melted butter
1 teaspoon lemon juice

Crust
2 cups flour
1 teaspoon salt
$^2/_3$ cup shortening
2 tablespoons butter
4 tablespoons ice water
Half-and-half, for glazing
Sugar, for sprinkling

(continued)

To Make Filling

1. Place blackberries, raspberries, and rhubarb in a large bowl. In a separate small bowl, mix together sugar and flour. Sprinkle sugar and flour mixture over fruit and gently mix just to combine. Cover bowl and refrigerate overnight.

To Make Crust

1. Mix together flour and salt in a large bowl. Cut in shortening and butter until mixture resembles coarse cornmeal.
2. Place one third of the flour mixture into a separate bowl and add water to form a paste. Pour paste into bowl with rest of flour and shortening and mix together to form dough into a ball. Form dough into a disc, wrap in plastic, and refrigerate for at least 20 minutes.
3. Divide dough in half and roll out one of the halves to fit into a 10-inch pie pan. Lay rolled dough into pie pan. Trim edges. Roll out remaining half of dough to fit over the pie. Refrigerate both crusts until ready to use.

To Bake Pie

Preheat oven to 400 degrees

1. Remove fruit from refrigerator and stir in melted butter and lemon juice. Pour filling into pie pan and place top crust over filling, crimping edges. Brush the top crust lightly with half and half, and sprinkle lightly with sugar.
2. Place pie in oven and bake for 10 minutes. Reduce oven temperature to 350 degrees and bake for 40 to 50 minutes more, until crust is golden brown. Remove from oven and cool slightly.

CARAMEL CUSTARD PIE
National Pie Championship

First Place, Custard and Pumpkin Category: Marles Riessland, Riverdale, Nebraska

This creamy and delicious pie is a real treat, but use caution when adding the hot milk to the liquified sugar to prevent splattering.

Makes one 10-inch pie

Crust
3 cups flour
1 teaspoon salt
1 teaspoon sugar
1 cup plus 1 tablespoon butter-flavored shortening, chilled
$^1/_3$ cup ice water
1 tablespoon white vinegar
1 large egg, well beaten

Filling
4 eggs
$^3/_4$ cup sugar
4 cups scalded milk
$^1/_4$ teaspoon salt
1 teaspoon vanilla
$^1/_8$ teaspoon nutmeg

(continued)

To Make Crust

1. Sift together flour, salt, and sugar into a mixing bowl. Cut in shortening with a pastry blender until mixture resembles cornmeal.

2. Combine water, vinegar, and egg and sprinkle, 1 tablespoon at a time, over flour mixture, tossing liquid and dry ingredients together with a fork to form a soft dough. Shape dough into 3 equal discs and wrap discs in plastic wrap. Refrigerate dough from 3 to 24 hours (any extra dough can be frozen for later use).

3. To prepare pie shell: Preheat oven 400 degrees. Roll one disk of dough out to fit a 10-inch pie shell. Lay dough into pie pan and trim and crimp edges. Line dough with a piece of aluminum foil, shiny side down, and fill pie shell with pie weights or uncooked beans. Place in oven and bake for 20 minutes. Remove the aluminum foil and weights, prick the crust thoroughly with a fork, and return pie shell to oven. Bake for an additional 5 to 10 minutes, or until crust is golden brown. Remove from oven and cool thoroughly. Keep oven on.

To Make Filling and Assemble Pie

1. Beat the eggs with $\frac{1}{4}$ cup of the sugar in medium bowl. Set aside.

2. In a small saucepan, cook the other $\frac{1}{2}$ cup of the sugar over medium-high heat, stirring, until sugar liquefies and becomes golden brown. Slowly stir in hot milk. Pour mixture into bowl with beaten eggs, salt, vanilla, and nutmeg. Stir to combine.

3. Pour filling into cooled pie crust and place in oven. Bake for 30–35 minutes or until set. Cool before serving.

NATIONAL
PIE
CHAMPIONSHIP

MUSHROOM SHERRY POT ROAST AND MUSHROOM POTATOES

Shelley Spud Day

First Place Winner, Championship Division: Clyde and Terryl Miller
This dish uses an interesting technique for flavoring by injecting the meat with sherry. Meat injectors can be purchased at specialty gourmet cookware stores.

Serves 4 to 6

One 2–3 pound beef roast
1 cup dry sherry
Seasoned meat tenderizer
3 tablespoons salad oil
$^3/_4$ pound mushrooms, sliced
$^1/_3$ cup water
1 bay leaf
$^1/_8$ teaspoon salt
16 baby red potatoes, peeled
2 tablespoons flour

1. Inject the roast with $^1/_2$ cup of the sherry and rub all over with meat tenderizer.

2. In a 14-inch, shallow Dutch oven (or any heavy pan suitable for braising), heat oil and brown roast on all sides to seal in juices. Add mushrooms, last $^1/_2$ cup of sherry, water, bay leaf, and salt to Dutch oven, stirring to combine. Cover and simmer for $2^1/_2$ to 3 hours, turning once, or until meat is fork tender.

3. While roast is cooking, prepare potatoes. Push a cylindrical apple corer halfway up into the center of each potato. Use a sharp knife to cut away the portion of the potato around the corer. Carefully remove the corer out of the potato and place the potato into ice water to stop discoloration. A half hour before serving, cook the potatoes in boiling salted water until just tender. Gently remove potatoes from cooking water, reserving 3 tablespoons of the water, and set aside.

(continued)

4. When roast is done remove from Dutch oven and keep warm.

5. In a cup, blend together flour and reserved cooking liquid. Gradually stir into the juices remaining in the Dutch oven and cook over medium-high heat, stirring, until sauce has thickened. Discard the bay leaf.

6. To serve, pour some of the gravy over the roast and pass the remaining gravy in a gravy boat. Serve with mushroom potatoes.

CRISPY POTATOES
Shelley Spud Day

These delicious, attractive potatoes are often served at Marcel Desaulniers' world-famous Trellis restaurant in historic Williamsburg, Virginia.

Serves 4

2 tablespoons vegetable oil
2 tablespoons clarified butter, melted
4 large Idaho baking potatoes
Salt and pepper, to taste

Preheat oven to 375 degrees

1. Combine the vegetable oil and clarified butter in a small bowl and stir to combine. Set aside.

2. Place the potatoes in a large saucepan and cover with cold water. Bring water to a boil, reduce heat, and simmer potatoes until they are just tender, about 1 hour.

3. Transfer the cooked potatoes to a plate and refrigerate until cool.

4. Cut the cooled potatoes in half with a serrated knife and then cut ¼ inch off each end. Slice the potatoes widthwise into thin slices and brush liberally with oil and butter mixture on both sides. Place slices on a baking sheet with sides and gently press each of the potato slices out to expose more potato, creating a shingled look. Season with salt and pepper. Place sheet on the middle rack of the oven and bake until brown and crispy, about 20 minutes.

PAPAS RELLENAS (STUFFED IDAHO POTATOES)
Shelley Spud Day

Courtesy of Chef Larry Kolar, Bolivar, New York City. These delicious stuffed potatoes require some extra work, but are well worth the effort. Be sure to refrigerate them before the final deep-frying.

Makes 12 stuffed potato cakes or 6 servings

6 medium Idaho potatoes (about 6 ounces each), peeled
$1/2$ medium onion, finely diced
2 cloves garlic, finely chopped
5 canned chipotle chilies, finely chopped (or more, to taste)
$1^1/2$ pounds extra lean ground beef
$1^1/2$ cups canned tomato sauce
Cumin, to taste
Salt and freshly ground black pepper, to taste
$1/2$ cup flour, for dredging
Oil, for frying

1. In a large saucepan, bring salted water to a boil. Cut potatoes into $1/4$-inch slices and cook until tender, about 10 minutes. Drain and let cool.

2. Add 1 or 2 tablespoons of oil to a medium skillet. Over medium heat, cook onion, garlic, and chipotle peppers until soft, about 8 minutes. Add beef and cook an additional 7 minutes or until the beef is browned and completely cooked through. Add tomato sauce and cook until thickened, about 8 minutes. Season with cumin, salt, and pepper.

3. Pass potatoes through a food mill and season with salt and pepper. With clean hands, form potatoes into approximately 12 balls, each about the size of a small lime. Roll balls in flour, covering them lightly on all sides.

4. Flatten the balls into "cakes" ¼ to ½-inch thick. Place approximately 1½ tablespoons of meat mixture in the center of each cake and then fold the cake up and over the filling, pinching to seal. Refrigerate stuffed potato cakes for 20 minutes.

5. Heat 2–3 inches of oil in a deep, heavy-bottomed pot over medium heat. (Oil should be 350 to 375 degrees.) Fry potato cakes until golden brown. Serve with salsa, if desired.

FRESH STRAWBERRY-CREAM CHEESE SPREAD

California Strawberry Festival

Strawberry spread is a real treat to serve with toasted bagels for a summer brunch. Reprinted from *The Totally Strawberry Cookbook* by Helene Siegal and Karen Gillingsworth (Celestial Arts).

Serves 6

1 cup stemmed, chopped strawberries
1 tablespoon sugar
One 8-ounce package cream cheese, softened
2 tablespoons heavy cream
1 teaspoon vanilla

1. Combine the strawberries and sugar in a small bowl and let sit for 5 minutes.
2. With an electric mixer, whip the cream cheese, heavy cream, and vanilla until light and fluffy. Gently fold in strawberries and mix just to combine. This spread will keep in the refrigerator for 2 days.

STRAWBERRY DUMPLINGS
California Strawberry Festival

Reprinted from *The Totally Strawberry Cookbook* by Helene Siegal and Karin Gillingham (Celestial Arts). This is a wonderful dish for any special occasion brunch.

Serves 4 to 6

5 to 6 cups strawberries, hulled and halved
$^3/_4$ cup sugar
1 cup all-purpose flour
$1^1/_2$ teaspoons baking powder
$^1/_4$ teaspoon baking soda
$^1/_4$ teaspoon salt
1 cup heavy cream
Additional sugar, for sprinkling

Preheat oven to 400 degrees

1. In a shallow, 2-quart casserole or baking dish combine strawberries and sugar. Place in oven.

2. While strawberries start to bake, mix together flour, baking powder, baking soda, and salt in a medium bowl. Stir in cream until batter is smooth.

3. When strawberry mixture begins to bubble, after about 8 minutes in the oven, remove from oven and drop large spoonfuls of the dumpling batter over the top, making about 8 dumplings. Sprinkle lightly with additional sugar. Place strawberries back in oven and bake until dumplings are puffy and golden, about 10 more minutes. Serve hot, or let cool slightly.

STRAWBERRY ROLY-POLY CHOCOLATE CAKE

California Strawberry Festival

Strawberries and chocolate rolled together in a cake. Who could ask for more? Reprinted from the *Totally Strawberry Cookbook* by Helene Siegal and Karen Gillingham (Celestial Arts).

Serves 8

Vegetable oil, for coating
$1/4$ cup cake flour
$1/4$ cup unsweetened cocoa powder
$1/4$ teaspoon baking soda
$1/4$ teaspoon salt
4 eggs, room temperature, separated
$1/2$ cup sugar
$1/4$ cup strawberry preserves
$1^1/2$ cups hulled and sliced strawberries
1 cup heavy cream, whipped
Whole strawberries, for garnish

Preheat oven to 400 degrees

1. Line a 15 x 10-inch jelly-roll pan with waxed or parchment paper. Lightly coat paper with vegetable oil.

2. Sift together flour, cocoa powder, baking soda, and salt into a medium bowl. Set aside.

3. In another medium bowl, beat the egg yolks with $1/4$ cup of the sugar, until egg yolks lighten in color, about 3 minutes.

4. In another medium bowl, whisk together egg whites until frothy. Gradually whisk in 2 tablespoons of the sugar until mixture becomes firm, about 1 minute longer.

(continued)

149

5. Stir one-third of the egg whites into the egg yolk mixture, then carefully fold in the rest of the egg whites. Fold in dry ingredients, one-third at a time. Spread batter in prepared pan and bake until center springs back when pressed, about 12 minutes. Remove from oven and cool for 10 minutes.

6. Sprinkle remaining sugar evenly over a 19 inch-long sheet of waxed paper. Turn cake out onto the prepared waxed paper and peel away paper lining in which cake was cooked. Starting at one long side, roll cake up in waxed paper. Twist ends of paper to secure and chill at least 3 hours.

7. To fill cake, remove from refrigerator and unroll on a work counter, resting cake on the paper. Spread preserves evenly over the cake. Sprinkle sliced strawberries evenly over preserves, leaving a 1-inch border along edges. Spread about two-thirds of the whipped cream over berries. Roll cake to enclose filling and wrap in waxed paper. Place on a tray, seam side down, and chill at least 1 hour longer.

8. To serve, unwrap cake from paper and place on a serving try. Frost with remaining whipped cream and garnish with whole strawberries. Cut in slices.

COOK-OFF AMERICA KITCHEN COURTESY OF WOOD-MODE

INDEX

ACKNOWLEDGEMENTS

The Cook-Off America television series and this companion cookbook were made possible by a number of companies and people with whom we are very proud to be associated.

It should be no surprise to anyone who grills that the Weber-Stephen Products Company would get behind a series that celebrates American regional cooking. Since the 1950s, Weber has single-handedly inspired American backyard cooks to new levels of greatness with their innovative and trend-setting products, including their kettle charcoal grills and their newer state-of-the-art gas grills. We are especially grateful to Michael Kempster, Sr., who first came up with the idea of a television series devoted to cook-offs. With his ongoing guidance and support, we benevolently regard him as the "father" of this project.

Just as a fine wine enhances any meal, Glen Ellen's sponsorship has been an enormous support to the series. The Glen Ellen Winery has been a true innovator and leader in the California wine-making community, showing just how good and affordable California wine can be. We'd like to give a special toast to Priscilla Felton and her staff at Glen Ellen whose support of the project has been invaluable.

We are also grateful to our sponsor, Celebrity Cruises, who truly understands the meaning of a culinary journey and has successfully proved it by offering the finest cuisine and wines in the cruise line industry, thanks to their superb chef, Michel Roux. Our special thanks to Celebrity staff John Husack and Helen Burford, whose accomplishments in the hospitality and travel industry demonstrate their tremendous vision and talents.

We are also delighted to have the support of Cascade and Procter & Gamble, a company that has been a household name for more than 100 years with the highest quality products that help people take care of both their families and homes. A special thank you to Kristen Nostrand, Jeff Keyser, and Lela Julius for their interest in and willingness to support Cook-off Amercia.

In our studio we were very fortunate to have two superb hosts, Marcel Desaulniers and Caprial Pence, who prepared the recipes from the festivals and cook-offs. Their knowledge and insights can inspire any cook --- experienced or not. We were also blessed with their ceaseless good humor and charm—both on and off the camera.

The exquisite kitchen set of Cook-Off America was provided by Wood-Mode, manufacturers of kitchen cabinetry. The brainchild of Bill Tobin and his team, it reflects the kind of beauty and unbeatable quality that has made Wood-Mode so successful. Our appliances were courtesy of another top-of-the-line name -- KitchenAid -- which graciously provided us both large and small kitchen appliances, along with their beautiful cookware. Our thanks to Brian Maynard for all his tremendous efforts and his ongoing support of our projects. We'd also like to thank Sur La Table for providing us with such beautiful props from their bountiful stores. A big thank you also to Eschenbach for their china, with their exquisite patterns and beautiful designs, which they kindly provided for the studio tapings.

We would also like to give a big thank you to the talented and hard-working staff at KCTS, the PBS station in Seattle where we taped the Cook-Off America programs.

Marjorie Poore
Alec Fatalevich
Producers

Cook-Off America © 2001 by Marjorie Poore Productions
Executive Chef: Brett Bailey
Photography: Alec Fatalevich

ISBN 0-9651095-8-5
Printed in Korea
10 9 8 7 6 5 4 3 2 1
MPP Books, 363 14th Avenue, San Francisco, CA 94118

NOTES

NOTES